THE REFERENCE SHELF (*Continued*)

THE REFERENCE SHELF

Vol. 22   No. 4

THE WELFARE STATE

Edited by
HERBERT L. MARX, Jr.
Associate Editor, Scholastic Magazines

THE H. W. WILSON COMPANY
NEW YORK   1950

1597

~~22696~~

PREFACE

This volume must begin—and end—on the level of questioning. Are we living in a welfare state now? Or is it a threat to or promise for the future? Is it compatible with or contradictory to the free enterprise system? Can it exist in harmony with a free representative democracy, or is it in conflict with our way of political life? Does it impair or strengthen the full, creative development of the individual? Can we afford the welfare state, or can we afford *not* to afford it?

To these questions this volume is directed. Yet we must operate under a grave handicap. People of all shades of opinion can agree on the definition (if not the merit) of a labor union, the United Nations, or the tariff. No such agreement has been reached on the definition of the welfare state. The first section of this volume introduces a series of definitions, all offered in good faith by men of serious intent. Yet many of these definitions contradict each other.

The task, however, is certainly worth tackling. For there is one strong theme which runs through the many variations of the welfare state discussion. Stepping in where many others have *not* feared to tread, we might express the basic theme this way: How much shall government do for its citizens, and how much shall individuals do for themselves? In searching for the way to progress and the better life for all, at what point shall we divide self-reliance from over-all action by the elected government?

These are questions, it might be noted, which can be realistically raised only in the United States and a few other nations. For in many countries even today, the vast majority of people have never known anything but the barest minimum level of existence. "Welfare" to them consists of food and shelter for the next day.

In another category entirely are those many countries with limited resources, particularly those struck body blows by World

War II. In these countries regulation by and reliance on a central government have been generally accepted, at least until some future time when new economic independence shall have been achieved.

The totalitarian countries of both left and right are in a third category. Here, unhappily, no argument is permitted. The state is all-powerful, dispensing or withholding whatever "welfare" it sees fit.

But in the United States we have the luxury of choice. Our phenomenal progress over the past century and a half may well seem minute in comparison with what the next century and a half will bring. Whether we choose greater or less direction and control by government, it seems reasonable to believe that we shall move forward to a healthier, fuller, more secure life. Will it be a freer life? That returns us to the nub of the welfare state argument.

This volume presents two major types of selections. The first consists of articles or speeches which have become "classics" in the welfare-state battle of words and ideas. These include selections by ex-President Hoover, James F. Byrnes, John Foster Dulles, Senator Herbert H. Lehman, Senator Paul H. Douglas, and spokesmen for the Truman Administration. The second type is made up of significant new approaches to the problem, often not directly "pro" or "con." It is hoped that these, especially, will throw light in some of the dark corners of the controversy which affects us all.

Acknowledgement is gratefully made to the many individuals and publishers for permission to reprint material. Such cooperation is basic in making this and other Reference Shelf volumes possible.

HERBERT L. MARX, JR.

July 9, 1950

CONTENTS

DANGERS OF THE WELFARE STATE

THE WELFARE STATE ABROAD

THE ESSENTIAL DILEMMA OF THE WELFARE STATE

The world has never had a good definition of the word "liberty," and the American people, just now, are much in need of one. We all declare for liberty; but in using the same word we do not all mean the same thing. With some the word "liberty" may mean for each man to do as he pleases with himself, and the product of his labor; while with others the same word may mean for some men to do as they please with other men, and the product of other men's labor. Here are two, not only different, but incompatible things, called by the same name, "liberty." And it follows that each of the things is, by the respective parties, called by two different and incompatible names—"liberty" and "tyranny."

ABRAHAM LINCOLN, speech at Baltimore, April 18, 1864.

FRAMEWORK OF THE PROBLEM

SOME DEFINITIONS

[The definitions of the welfare state which follow enable any reader, regardless of what preconceived notions he may bring to them, to find at least one that pleases him. They demonstrate, in capsule form, how difficult it will be to find general areas of agreement on the subject. Unless otherwise noted, the quotations are from selections which may be found in this volume.—Editor.]

[The welfare state] describes a system under which a ruling class of bureaucrats claims to be able to spend the citizen's own money much more usefully than he can.—*Saturday Evening Post, November 19, 1949.*

The welfare state is a society in which an assured minimum standard of living and opportunity becomes the possession of every citizen.—*G. D. H. Cole, British Socialist scholar, quoted in Labor and Nation, Winter, 1949-50.*

A series of acts and agencies which provide services for people in an age of interdependence and mass production, which most people cannot provide for themselves.—*Stuart Chase.*

I say service state rather than welfare state. The term welfare state seems to me a boast. . . The service state, the state which, instead of preserving peace and order and employing itself with maintaining the general security, takes the whole domain of human welfare for its province and would solve all economic and social ills through its administrative activities, has been creeping up on us.—*Roscoe Pound, dean emeritus, Harvard University Law School, in "The Rise of the Service State."*

The welfare state is simply a state in which people are free to develop their individual capacities, to receive just awards for their talents, and to engage in the pursuit of happiness, unburdened by fear of actual hunger, actual homelessness or oppression by reason of race, creed, or color.—*Senator Herbert H. Lehman of New York.*

The welfare state is a new phrase for an old theory of government under which government officials assume responsibility for the material welfare of the people.—*Robert S. Byfield, member, New York Stock Exchange.*

The welfare state . . . is a system wherein government agrees to underwrite certain levels of employment, income, education, medical aid, social security, and housing for all its citizens.—*Arthur Schlesinger, Jr., historian.*

The welfare state is a government which ceases to rely on the individual and takes general responsibility in providing economic security, health, and general well-being of its citizens. —*Senior Scholastic, October 5, 1949.*

It must have been some very clumsy Republican—I do not know the origin of the phrase or who perpetrated it—who tried to pin the label "welfare state" on Mr. Truman's government. Others joined in the clamor and, of course, the apologists for big government joyously accepted the epithet as a new instrument of party warfare. They admit they are running a welfare state. They are proud of it!

Of course, they are running a welfare state. There has never been a responsible government which did not have the welfare of its people at heart. I am proud of the fact that we in the state of New York have made great social welfare advances, as have most of the states.

Anybody who thinks that an attack on the fundamental idea of security and welfare is appealing to people generally, is living in the Middle Ages.—*Governor Thomas E. Dewey of New York, from a political science lecture delivered at Princeton University, condensed in U. S. News & World Report, February 24, 1950.*

150 YEARS OF THE WELFARE STATE [1]

In 1800 William Henry Harrison, the delegate from the Northwest Territory, lobbied through Congress a law which, in effect, put the Federal Government into the mortgage business. At that moment the welfare state, which today often looks like a modern creation, had arrived.

Harrison's act cut fom $200 to $2 an acre the price at which the government was authorized to sell western public lands to settlers, and it gave the buyer four years to buy the land, provided he made a down payment of one fourth the price. The government held the settler's note those four years.

The powers which that modest law conferred on the Federal Government—just then setting up shop in Washington after its move from Philadelphia—threw the young nation into a raging controversy about the role of the state in economic transactions. The government credit scheme cut into the business of western bankers, who had been financing the purchase of farms by new settlers. And it hurt New England manufacturers, because it gave their labor a bargaining lever for higher pay. When no raise was forthcoming, the workman could always head west and make a farmer of himself with Washington's help.

After a hundred and fifty years, the controversy has become an American tradition. It still rages, because the United States rests on two ideas that never will be at ease with one another—"property" vs. "equality." Each of those incompatible ideas comes out of the roots of the nation. Each had strong advocates when the founders of the republic were writing the Constitution.

As early as 1772, Samuel Adams of Massachusetts had stated the natural rights of the colonists to be, "first, a right to life; secondly, to liberty; thirdly, to property." Those of his school preached that a government which would safeguard individual profit and private property was the key to the well-being of every American.

Another sect, which included Jefferson, wanted a system of government that would protect the idea of equality which

[1] From an article by Blair Bolles, of the Foreign Policy Association. *Nation's Business*. 38:33-4+. April 1950. Reprinted by permission.

the Declaration of Independence had expressed in the words, "life, liberty and the pursuit of happiness." So far the government has preserved equality principally by controlling property.

The controversy is profound because at stake is man's conception of freedom. The constitutionalists protest that government interference limits the freedom of individuals to work out their own economic destinies. The equalitarians insist that full freedom in business limits the freedom of persons not in business to provide for their own economic well-being. If it is not possible for everybody to be completely free at the same time, is it the duty of government to take a measure of freedom from one person to enhance the freedom of another? On that question America seethes.

The wording of the Constitution represented a victory for the friends of freedom in enterprise. But, by statutes and White House decisions, the equalitarians have been progressively diluting that victory. After a long period of slow progress, they have dominated American political life in the twentieth century.

The essence of the American welfare state which the equalitarians have developed is a paradox. To keep the various segments of the country's population in rough balance, the Federal Government singles out special groups for unequal treatment under law—farmers, industrial labor and consumers. As it pushes forward those groups, Washington pulls back others.

President Andrew Jackson set the precedent for pulling back almost a hundred and twenty years ago when he refused to renew the charter of the United States Bank. Thus he destroyed the bank's grip on credit and currency policy, the control of which displeased the settlers whom Harrison's land law had attracted to the West.

The Federal Government has relied mainly on four devices to keep the economic relations of the various segments of America in flexible relationship with one another. Device No. 1 is the subsidy. Until the high tide of westward migration closed the frontier, Washington distributed subsidies in the form of land. The income tax has enabled the Federal Government to subsidize with cash.

Device No. 2 is the statute conferring special privileges on a particular group to strengthen it in rivalry with other groups (the Wagner Act protecting labor's privilege of organizing is the best example). Device No. 3 is the administrative agency which supervises the conduct of business. And device No. 4 is the general law, like the Social Security Act or the Minimum Wage Law, designed to guard the personal welfare of those who rely on their muscle or their wits and not on property to provide them with an income.

The welfare state activities are different from other undertakings by which the Federal Government interferes with the natural workings of economics. By administering the protective tariff, Washington has affected profoundly the nature of the United States. But the country originally regarded protection as a means for promoting the "general" welfare—that is, the welfare of all—in one single stroke. It was meant to benefit farmers, factory owners, and farm and factory labor. The early Senator Robert LaFollette of Wisconsin, one of the architects of the modern welfare state, strongly defended protection in Congress as a device of universal beneficence, although years afterward he denounced it as an undesirable source of more wealth for the wealthy. Federal subsidies for road building fall into the "general" welfare category of the tariff, as does the mail subsidy on periodicals.

Until Theodore Roosevelt's day, farmers in the West almost alone stoked the welfare fires. They heated Andrew Jackson and Abraham Lincoln, who let himself be diverted from the Civil War long enough to push successfully for enactment of the Homestead Law and the Morrill Act. The Homestead Law went further than Harrison's law. It donated the public land to settlers. Under the Morrill Act, the Federal Government gave away more land, for the establishment of colleges of agriculture.

But the city-dwelling abolitionists were responsible for Lincoln's most sweeping contribution to equality—the Emancipation Proclamation which freed from slavery the three and a half million Negroes in the Confederate States. The Proclamation and Northern victory in the Civil War led to adoption three years after Lincoln's assassination of the Fourteenth and Fifteenth Amendments through which Northern "radicals" tried to confirm the rights of Negroes to political and judicial equality with white Americans.

Congress was trying to satisfy indignant farmers when it established the Interstate Commerce Commission—the first of the federal administrative agencies. William Jennings Bryan drew his inspiration from the unrest of farmers when he ran for the presidency in the closing days of the nineteenth century on a cheap money platform. By that time the free land opportunities in the West were narrowing. Washington had sold or given away a great portion of the public land. Then the insecure began to count on the Federal Government instead of new green pastures for their personal security. The "pluck-and-luck," "root-hog-or-die" notions prevalent at the high tide of rugged individualism in the 1880s began to pale.

In the midst of the discontent flowing from Americans unable to seek their fortunes along some new Oregon trail, Theodore Roosevelt introduced the United States to the first twentieth century model of the welfare state. Soon after he took the presidential oath September 14, 1901, he began to hear a clamor for Washington to curb the great bankers and the managers of the largest corporations. A strange phenomenon was taking place. Businessmen had attained so much power that many people, uncertain of their own economic footing, had begun to fear them.

In that frame of mind, Americans discussed seriously whether any man who possessed a billion dollars was not a menace to the nation. The muckrakers exposed the sins of big business in detail. In the farm states of the far Midwest, reformers like Governor LaFollette of Wisconsin were trimming the power of the railroads—which always looked like the devil on wheels to the farmers who put LaFollette into office—and were using the Federal Government to protect the farmer and the consumer from whims of other mighty free enterprise.

Business men readily acknowledged their own power. . . . In such an atmosphere, the Republican Roosevelt came to envision Washington as the protector of the weak and the chastiser of the unruly strong, whom he called "malefactors of great wealth." So he successfully urged Congress to establish a Bureau of Corporations, which would keep tabs on the expansions of business concerns. He curbed the power of the railroads by persuading Congress to authorize the Interstate Commerce Commission to set rates. He protected the consumer with a Pure Food Law and a Meat Inspection Law, which diluted the freedom of the packers.

While Roosevelt sponsored few other such measures, his administration showed that it is difficult for a President to ignore demands for equalitarian legislation when numerically strong groups want it. The colleagues of Joseph G. Cannon, Speaker of the House in Roosevelt's administration, deprived him of his great powers because he refused to heed the requests of the discontented for federal favors. America's institutions for self-government cannot neglect the cry for equality when it is loud. The modern welfare state is the creation of twentieth century political pressures.

The momentum generated under Roosevelt lasted until the United States entered the war against Germany in 1917. The issue of the welfare state created such a ruckus among the Republicans that they split in the presidential election of 1912, and the Democrat Woodrow Wilson won the highest office. The modern era actually begins with his administration.

Wilson became President almost simultaneously with the adoption of the income tax amendment to the Constitution and the levy has been the major tool in the construction of the welfare state as we know it today.

Like Andrew Jackson, Wilson was preoccupied with abuses in the conduct of business and with the claims of farmers to special help from the whole nation. The new President's contributions to the furtherance of the welfare state idea had a novel origin, because he depended on an intellectual, Louis D. Brandeis, for guidance in putting the idea to work. Brandeis was the first brain truster.

Wilson first attended to business. At his request, Congress passed the Clayton Act, which gave the President new powers to break up combinations in restraint of trade, and created the Federal Trade Commission, an administrative agency, as a sort of prefect of discipline over business.

Wilson began to dispense the government largess among farmers after Congress passed the income tax law (embedded in the Underwood-Simmons Tariff) in 1913. The subsidies flowed out of the Treasury down the chutes provided in the Smith-Lever Act, which financed agrarian mortgages.

The steam behind the equalitarian movement weakens periodically, when the nation is distracted by larger issues or when government action has corrected the examples of economic imbalance that are striking enough to create a political power drive on Washington. Interest in the welfare state was shot away by World War I and did not revive from the end of Wilson's presidency until twelve years afterward, when Franklin D. Roosevelt brought his New Deal to Washington.

The Democratic Roosevelt gave four original twists to the welfare state. He introduced the idea of national planning as he tried to fit together a series of schemes for helping the various groups laid low by the depression. But the national economy refused to fit neatly into a plan, which seldom works satisfactorily even in Socialist countries, where the government itself can make all the decisions about economics. Roosevelt quietly gave up planning and followed his predecessors' custom of helping different groups independently of one another.

His other novelties survived longer. He was the first welfare state President, for example, who cemented a close political alliance between the White House and organized labor.

Presidents in the past had responded to union pressures by introducing the eight-hour law in federal offices, cutting immigration, and, in the case of Wilson, partially exempting labor from the antitrust laws. Wilson had tried to outlaw child labor, but the courts said his legislation was unconstitutional.

On the eve of Franklin Roosevelt's election, two Republicans, Senator George Norris of Nebraska and Representative Fiorello La Guardia of New York, strengthened labor's bargaining position by pushing through Congress and into the United States Code their act forbidding the issurance of court injunctions in labor disputes. But Roosevelt's Wagner Act and the Minimum Wage Law became the portals through which labor entered into the inner sanctum of the welfare state.

Another original contribution by Roosevelt was his method of financing the cost of welfare state undertakings. His budgets provided for spending more than the treasury took in, as he assumed on behalf of the Federal Government the novel responsibility of giving work to the unemployed. That was the fourth twist he gave to the welfare state. The sum of his activities dramatized statism as a national way of life.

The result of that dramatization still colors America. Today the political roots of the welfare state seem to lie deeper than ever.

New Deal philosophy faded during World War II, although the government controlled severely many aspects of Americans' private and business lives. When the war ended, Harry Truman, the new President, showed only casual interest in equalitarianism. To suggestions that he build a new wing of the welfare state on the foundations of wartime price control he paid little heed, and price control ended. He said he would break up a threatened railway strike by drafting the strikers into the army. By 1948 he had balanced the budget. But he soon decided that, politically, he was pleasing the wrong people.

Moreover, his ancestors and he alike have felt at close range the growth of the idea from its simple applications into that complex institution, the contemporary executive branch of the Federal Government, costing $42 billion a year to operate, over which the President presides.

His two great-grandmothers, Nancy Tyler and Emily Shippe, went over the mountains from Virginia to Kentucky. That migration carried the seeds of the welfare state. From Kentucky the families pushed on to Missouri where the President's grandfather, Solomon Young, made money by outfitting movers setting out toward a promised land at the end of the Oregon or Santa Fe trail. The movers were trying to provide for their own welfare but, by the end of the nineteenth century, opportunities to move were narrowing.

So, responding to his own tradition and to political reality Truman, in 1948, turned back to the welfare state. He campaigned with the philosophy of Jackson, Theodore Roosevelt, Wilson and Franklin Roosevelt when he ran for the presidency that year.

"We cannot maintain prosperity unless we have a fair distribution of opportunity," he said.

His instinct was correct. He won the election.

Yet welfare state opponents have not become politically helpless. While presidents consult the equalitarians, congressmen have a way of consulting the constitutionalists. It is not every day that Congress plays the welfare tune as it did last summer [1949] in passing the Low-Cost Housing Act and the new Minimum Wage Law at the behest of Harry Truman. More often Congress is in the mood it shows when it refuses to enact a federal health insurance act.

To the gulf between President and Congress that characterizes American political life in almost every year of the republic's history, business probably owes its survival in relative independence.

Although the equalitarians' advance means that the opponents of government interference in the economic and social life of the country have been slowly retreating from the high ground on which the authors of the Constitution set them, they can take heart from the history of a hundred and fifty years. The private enterprising American began to show his ingenuity in pioneer days by erecting a solid civilization in a wilderness. He has shown the same ingenuity in more difficult circumstances by adapting himself and pretty well overcoming the hazards thrown in his way by government under the guidance of the equalitarians.

The period of swiftest advance of the welfare idea—from Franklin D. Roosevelt's first inauguration—also has been the period of greatest expansion of the productive economy, under the management of private enterprise. While controls have lengthened, profits have mounted. Business has shown that it can rise to the challenge of the welfare state movement and assure its own survival by its ability to operate in the shadow of this threat to business incentives.

The pattern of American economic activity is immensely different from what it was when Theodore Roosevelt launched his Square Deal. It has changed strikingly also since Wilson initiated the New Freedom, since Franklin Roosevelt unrolled his New Deal, and even since Truman developed his Fair Deal. But the foundation of economic life remains private enterprise, even if it is not completely free enterprise. The welfare state polices business but seldom manages it.

But to survive in freedom, business has grown large, to satisfy an equalitarian urge of its own. In bigness business has sought strength to save itself from domination by big government. As business grows, however, the sponsors of welfare statism see new reasons for government to grow. And each advance in power achieved by the government makes more acute the question whether by empowering the state to save us, we are putting the state in a position ultimately to swallow us.

A JOURNEY THROUGH THE WELFARE STATE [2]

I have been asking people in various walks of life—taxi drivers, bankers, bell boys, lawyers, housewives, barbers, red caps—what the term "welfare state" means to them. . . .

To about half my "sample"— admittedly sadly lacking in scientific rigor—the term meant nothing at all. "No sir," said a waitress in a station lunchroom, "I never heard of it." To others it meant something pretty nice; to about the same number, something pretty evil. "Coddling labor . . . mortgaging your child's future . . . something for nothing . . . destroying initiative and the American Way. . . ." A few tough-minded souls identified it with "old-age pensions," or "farm subsidies," and proceeded to pass judgment on that.

Most of those who had an opinion looked at the welfare state as an entity, something alive and kicking out there in the

[2] From an article by Stuart Chase, economist and author. *Nation's Business.* 38:39-40+. May 1950. Reprinted by permission.

space-time world. They divided, however, between seeing a dark and ominous monster, and a luminous ectoplasm radiating cheer.

This checks in a general way with another one-man poll I ran on the term "fascism," before the war. Nearly every one of the hundred persons who had an opinion—many did not— saw fascism as a substantial entity, but no two saw it the same way. I got a hundred different definitions. . . .

When it comes to welfare state, I tag along with the people in my one-man poll who named a specific agency, like the Social Security Administration. For my money . . . the welfare state is a label to cover a large number of services provided by the community for its citizens, most of which are paid for by direct or indirect taxation. I find it impossible to have any useful opinions about the label until I take a careful look at the services it covers.

If somebody wants to define welfare state as a condition where citizens demand more goods while producing less, obviously such a situation makes no sense in the long run; the economy will collapse. If he wants to define it as a condition where everyone gets his just deserts, obviously it is Utopia, and pretty dubious of realization. The definition I elect, and the common one from the semantic point of view, is a verbal label for a series of acts and agencies which provide services for people in an age of interdependence and mass production, which most people cannot provide for themselves.

What are these services in the America of 1950? . . . We can readily write down perhaps a hundred agencies, past, present and proposed, coming under the head of the general welfare. They can then be classified by functions, something like this:

Educational welfare: the public school system, land grant colleges, state aid to local schools, federal aid to states, the GI Bill of Rights as applied to education, and so on.

Health: the Public Health Service, Veterans Administration hospitals, public clinics, workmen's compensation laws, sanitation measures, pure food and drug legislation, milk inspection, stream pollution abatement, the proposal for health insurance, the Red Cross, and so on.

Child welfare: the Child Labor Law, public playgrounds, state aid to blind and crippled children, school lunch programs, public day nurseries, etc.

Old people: old-age pensions under the Social Security Act of 1935—the insurance feature; old-age "assistance" under the same Act—the charity feature; state relief; county poor farms, etc.

People out of work: unemployment insurance, the U. S. Employment Service; the WPA, PWA and CCC of the 1930s.

Working conditions: factory inspection, minimum-wage laws, mine inspection, silicosis prevention, etc.

Shelter: building inspection, rent controls, FHA loans, Federal and state housing projects, slum clearance, GI housing loans, etc.

Farmers: the Homestead Act, parity price supports, farm credit agencies, AAA, the Food Stamp Plan, the Soil Conservation Service, the fertilizer program of the TVA, and so on.

Labor unions: anti-injunction laws, the Wagner Act, the Taft-Hartley Act, the Federal Conciliation Service, and plenty more.

Industry: highways provided free for the trucking business, subsidies to airlines for carrying the mails, postal subsidies to magazines, newspapers and book publishers, subsidies to the merchant marine, RFC loans to banks, insurance companies and business enterprises like Lustron, the protective tariff as a subsidy to many industries.

General supervision and protection: antitrust laws, the Federal Trade Commission and Clayton Act, Securities and Exchange Commission, the insuring of bank deposits through the FDIC, the Interstate Commerce Commission, the Federal Communications Commission, the Federal Power Commission, and so on and so forth.

This is not the full list by a long shot. It includes some services which have been discontinued, like the WPA, some that are only proposed, like federal aid to local schools, but most of them are current and going strong. . . .

Certainly no American is against them all. Yet plenty are passionately for or against the abstract term.

As one goes down the list, adding a date now and then, one realizes that most of them originated in response to a need, sometimes, like the Homestead Act and unemployment insurance, a roaring, driving need. Even the tariff filled an important need at a critical time when new industries were being established and needed protection. There is a reason for every item on the list and often a pretty good reason.

Some people will line up against aid to farmers; some farmers may line up against help to unions; some unions may line up against subsidies to industry—but how many of us are against aid to blind and crippled children, against pure food and drugs, against conservation, land grant colleges, and the Homestead Act? When we get down to earth where pictures can be taken, emotion evaporates and critical evaluation comes in. On this level nobody is against the welfare state in toto, and nobody is for it. . . .

Suppose we take a service falling under the head of the general welfare—one which shares the headlines today with the H-bomb. As medical science expands the life span, problems of the aged in a high-energy society become ever more acute.

J. W. Myers, who figures out the pension system of the Standard Oil Company of New Jersey, in an article in the *Harvard Business Review*,[3] says that the demand for economic security is world wide, is growing, and while it may be regretted, it cannot be ignored. Sooner or later, he says, "men take steps to protect themselves from what they fear."

Jersey Standard set up its first pension plan in 1903, and has had almost fifty years of experience, so Myers is not talking through his hat. The policy of this company now is based on a partnership between public and private pension systems.

[3] Myers, J. M. Governmental and voluntary programs for security. *Harvard Business Review*. 28:29-44. March 1950.

The Federal Government should meet basic needs, and private employers, wherever possible, should *supplement* that base with what might be called a "comfort" standard, giving the retired worker a pension not too far below his average income in his active years.

Other Jersey principles are: Joint contributions by employee and company; mandatory retirement at sixty-five to keep the company "young" and its operations efficient; the "vesting" principle whereby the employee does not lose the right to his pension when he leaves the company for any reason; uniform treatment for employees and executives; flexibility to meet changing price levels and conditions and checking all changes in the plan with employees.

Ninety-eight per cent of Jersey workers are participating in the plan, and are almost unanimous in their praise of it, according to opinion polls. Meanwhile labor turnover is low, morale is high, and a glance at Jersey's earnings shows that somebody is showing plenty of initiative. Management feels that old-age security, far from causing workers to coast and dawdle, has the opposite effect. Indeed, Dr. Sumner Slichter, the distinguished economist, points out that if a man feels that his old age is reasonably secure, he may be willing to take more risks in venture capital enterprises.

The Jersey plan is government "welfare" combined with company "welfare," a combination we are likely to see much more of. The management likes it, the workers like it, doubtless the Social Security Administration is pleased. Frank W. Pierce, a director of Standard Oil Company, in a talk to a management group makes an eloquent case for provisions against economic insecurity under machine-age conditions:

"Men and women want security—security for themselves and for their families . . . against sudden onslaughts of the unexpected, against illness, disease, death, loss of earning power, depression and old age."

Since 1919, says Pierce, people punching a time clock have increased 60 per cent, while the number of the self-employed has not increased at all! What a lesson in these figures! In a rural economy the farmer and craftsman have some control over their economic destiny. The machine-age worker is at the mercy of forces beyond his control, and often beyond the control of his employer. War, inflation, depression, industrial shifts, unemployment, a crippling accident, a major operation for his wife —what blow may not fall next?

It may be objected that the employee ought to save a competence for his declining years, as well as for other emergencies, without help from either government or employer. But to provide an annuity of $100 a month at age sixty-five means he must save $15,000 over his working years! This is quite beyond the power of the average worker with a family to rear. . . .

Besides, if . . . workers, began to save in a big way, what would happen to sales of television sets, washing machines, parlor furniture, radios and new cars? We Americans have a stern duty as consumers.

In 1900 there were only about three million Americans sixty-five or older. Mostly they lived with their relatives in rural areas, and were no great problem. Now we have eleven million and often there is no room to double up with relatives in cold-water flats. By 1980, the way things are going, we will have twenty-two million. As Myers says, there is no ignoring a problem of this dimension; it must be faced.

Somehow old people must be taken care of. Only societies which are seriously short of food ceremoniously kill the aged. A pension is the most honorable and decent way to care for them in our society. Can we afford it? Dr. Slichter in the New York *Times* for October 16, 1949, calculates that 8 per cent of the United States payrolls will be needed for an adequate if modest pension. United States production, he says, has been increasing some 2 per cent a year on the average. If this rate can be maintained, production will be up some 80 per cent in the next thirty years. Hence, he says, the cost of old-age security may not be more than one tenth of the gain in production. Production, of course, is the key.

"A great nation," remarked the London *Economist* recently, "can afford anything it can produce." It looks as though there was room to turn around in, if production continues to rise. The fifty years' experience of Jersey Standard indicates that a pension system helps rather than hinders production.

The above are a few of the issues involved in just *one* of the activities included under the verbal blanket of the welfare state. We touched on public and private interlocking systems, incentives, risk taking, mass demand, size of annuities, the increasing life span, interdependence, gross and net costs. There are plenty of other angles.

Returning to the list of agencies, of which pensions are but a single example, it is possible, of course, to make a similar highlight inventory of each. . . . A truly gigantic task is involved, altogether too much for one man. There are, however, some general statements one can make about the list without violating, I think, the underlying facts.

1. Every agency originated in popular demand, not in ideological manipulation. The British Labor party is now engaged in nationalizing some industries for purely ideological reasons. Our list contains no single case of this. Americans were landless, jobless, sick or broke or scared. Industies were deep in the red. Philip H. Willkie, in a letter to the New York *Herald Tribune*, puts it this way:

"Most of the American people are not concerned with an overwhelming fear of socialism, statism or the welfare state. They are concerned with living. They think about the things which affect their own lives—their take-home pay, their rent, their grocery bill, the kind of house in which they live, how to pay for a major operation, and what is going to happen to them when they get old."

2. Feelings of insecurity which led to these mass demands are primarily the result of transition from a handicraft culture to a high-energy culture. Two world wars have added their quota of uncertainty, while the black days of 1933 with fifteen million unemployed have burned into the mind of every worker who lived through them.

3. In our complicated, interdependent culture, furthermore, many services are mandatory for survival, which the industrial worker, and now even the farmer, cannot provide unaided. Such

services appear in the list above—public schools, public health, traffic controls, factory inspection, conservation, flood control, protection of children, care of the aged. No modern state would dare operate without these safeguards.

4. Finally, we can be quite sure that no agency on the list, past or present, is without defect in its design, in its administration, or both. Every function could be done more effectively and at a lower cost. . . .

If we really want to do something constructive about the welfare state, the path is clear. Stop crying "Up with it" or "Down with it" and begin analyzing. I have given a rough analysis of pensions, but a much more thorough study is needed before conclusions can be reached and useful action taken.

AT THE LEVEL OF THE STATES [4]

[This discussion of 1949 state legislation includes many proposals which were never voted upon or even fully debated. The intention is simply to show the variety of welfare proposals being considered at the state level.—Editor]

During the past decade and a half, the concept of the "welfare state" has assumed an increasingly significant place in the social and political thinking of America, and has profoundly influenced the fiscal policies of government. . . .

Almost invariably, this broad concept is linked with the growth of the Federal Government. Almost invariably also, it speaks in large social values and minimizes economic values. The New Deal of Franklin Roosevelt and the Fair Deal of Harry Truman are two facets of the movement which in its dramatic impact has dwarfed into insignificance the welfare activities of the 150,000 units of state and local government in the United States. Recent appraisals are, therefore, concerned almost exclusively with the activities of the national government —a natural reflection of the sheer magnitude and scope of

[4] From "The 'Welfare State' at the State Level," by John F. Sly, director, Princeton Surveys. *Tax Review*, publication of the Tax Foundation. 10:27-32. June 1949. Reprinted by permission.

federal expenditures and of the compelling position Washington has evidenced in such areas as social insurance and public power.

At the national level today, attention is focused on Administration proposals calling for an extension of the welfare state. . . . But the predominant role of the Federal Government has by no means precluded significant developments at the state level. Both recent and current legislative activity may point to a resurgence of state initiative in new areas such as cash sickness benefits and to the expansion of old and accepted services such as education and public health. Stimulated and even alarmed by an ever-emerging federal dominance, and with an eye cocked expectantly toward an "election year," states are embarking upon or are considering new and significant programs in the welfare field.

A recent factual survey has been made by the Tax Foundation of welfare state activities in twenty-eight states covering the period from the beginning of their 1949 legislative sessions through the first week of April [1949]. This preliminary survey was not intended to be definitive, but it covers activities in ten broad categories. . . .

Compulsory Health Insurance: The survey reveals that bills providing for compulsory health insurance have been introduced in four states—California, Connecticut, Rhode Island, and Wisconsin. In California two important bills have been presented to the legislature. Both call for extensive services including medical, surgical, dental, and hospital care. Costs of the plan would be borne jointly by the employer and employee. It is significant that the governor of California sponsored a health insurance measure four years ago and that an interim committee also recommended such legislation.

The health insurance proposal that has been made in Rhode Island would also involve joint financing by employer and employee. In the Connecticut proposal costs would be borne by the employer alone.

In Wisconsin measures have been introduced by members of both parties, providing for health insurance to cover non-job-connected accidents and sickness. One bill would require coverage by a compulsory state-administrated plan, while another would permit the alternative of private insurance.

Cash Sickness Benefit Programs: In this new area three states had already enacted legislation—Rhode Island, California, and New Jersey. This year New York and Washington have enacted cash sickness benefit programs. The New York law allows the employer the option of insuring with private insurance carriers or of self-insurance in the state fund. The Washington act calls for a one per cent payroll deduction, but also allows insuring under a comparable private group plan.

In Massachusetts the governor recommended a system of compulsory health insurance for industrial workers and their families "to provide our people with cash sickness benefits and insure their receiving adequate medical care." In Minnesota two bills have been introduced which provide a schedule of benefits to individuals who are disabled or ill, the amount and length of benefits comparable to unemployment compensation payments. One bill provides for a one per cent payroll tax on the employee, and the other provides for one half of one per cent each from employer and employee.

Public Housing: This activity seems to be of significance in seventeen of the twenty-eight states, with action ranging from the proposal stage in Massachusetts and Michigan to enactments in Kentucky, New York, and Wisconsin. For the most part, the legislation calls for appropriations or bond issues to aid in constructing low-cost housing.

In New Jersey a special session of the legislature has referred the question of a $100 million bond issue to provide "safe and sanitary" housing in blighted and substandard areas to the voters in the November [1949] election.

In California eighty-five bills were before the legislature which dealt in some manner with public housing, none of which had passed both houses by April 8. Part of the proposals are to be carried out by a community development program and agency, and administered by anticipated federal funds. In November 1948, the voters defeated a program for $100 million of state housing by about two to one (which may reflect the attitude of many voters who demand services but who are reluctant to foot the bill).

In New York three bills sponsored by the administration were passed to submit three housing propositions to the voters at the 1949 general election. One of the bills authorizes a $300 million housing bond issue; the second increases the maximum annual subsidy amount payable by the state from $14 million to $25 million; and the third permits the state to contract in any one year for subsidy payments up to $2.5 million instead of $1.5 million.

Old Age Pensions: Pensions to all aged persons without regard to need have been proposed in three states. In Connecticut a $173 million a year old age pension has been introduced, but apparently without any substantial backing. In Missouri a similar proposal is likewise considered unlikely to pass. The estimated annual cost of this proposal is $185 million (total state expenditures in 1947 were $157 million). In Montana a bill was killed which would have resulted in an increase in old age assistance payments to $100 per month, at a total annual cost of some $85 million.

Public Assistance: In twenty of the twenty-eight states, legislatures have dealt with major proposals in the public assistance field; seven states have passed legislation. Arizona has enacted a proposal estimated to cost an additional $1 million annually (in addition to October 1948 legislation which increased public assistance costs by $3 million annually). In Arkansas state appropriations for public welfare purposes for the 1949-1951 biennium have been increased by 67 per cent over the current biennium. In Illinois a new feature has been added in old age and blind assistance payment ceilings; a compromise to the complete removal of ceilings is an act providing $65 per month with a sliding maximum, to be adjusted up or down semi-annually in the amount of a dollar for each three full points of change occurring in the Consumers' Price Index for Chicago. In New Jersey a concurrent resolution passed the Assembly memorializing Congress to increase the federal contribution for old age assistance.

Unemployment Compensation: The survey reveals that significant legislation has been introduced in nineteen states on the subject of unemployment compensation and its expansion. Most of the proposals call for increases in weekly benefits of $2 to $5 with some as high as $10 (Illinois and Michigan). The greatest that has been enacted into law is a $5 increase in Minnesota and Wyoming.

Other proposals would provide for an extension of unemployment compensation to groups of workers not covered at the present time. One bill was killed in Montana which provided for extending coverage to farm workers. In Massachusetts a legislative commission has recommended that coverage be extended to state and local government employees; a similar proposal has been made in Connecticut. California proposals would cover the same two groups plus domestic servants.

Bills introduced in Connecticut, Illinois and New York would provide for unemployment compensation payments to persons idle because of labor disputes.

Education: At least nine of the states covered in the survey have been considering major legislation on education. Many of the proposed bills would cover adult, vocational and higher education; several covered such items as school lunch programs. Several bills in California propose free lunches to all school children; one would include school employees in the free lunch program. In Minnesota bills have been introduced which would authorize local school districts to construct or purchase homes for teachers. In New York the program to establish a state university, including community colleges with state aid, was advanced this year with an appropriation of $12 million.

Public Health: At least twelve of the state legislatures have been considering proposals in the public health area. Many of these would call for the expansion of existing services. In Wisconsin, however, there is a bill pending which would appropriate state funds to be used as a subsidy, up to $1,800 each, to en-

courage doctors to move into rural areas; this proposal has the
support of the state medical society. In Connecticut a bill has
been introduced providing scholarships for the training of
nurses at state expense, at an estimated annual cost of $450,000.

Hospitals and Institutions: Bills or acts in thirteen states call
for marked expansion in this activity. Many proposals, such as
those in California, are concerned with mental cases, cancer
patients, and alcoholics. In Idaho and Wyoming acts have been
passed authorizing increases in property tax levies for support
of county hospitals. In New Jersey the legislature passed an act
providing for a referendum on a $25 million bond issue for new
construction and improvement of existing facilities in state hospitals and other institutions; a 1948 law was extended for another two years permitting all municipalities not having municipal hospitals to determine amounts of appropriations needed to
be made for private charitable hospitals, both for treatment of
indigent patients and for general support of private hospitals.

Miscellaneous: Miscellaneous bills in nine states covered such
items as the establishment of Merrimack Valley Authorities
(New Hampshire); child care centers (California and New
York); child guidance centers (New Jersey), and state youth
commissions (Illinois and Wyoming). In Kentucky a proposal
was made by the Mayor of the City of Louisville to buy the
Louisville Railway Company. The income was to go to the
University of Louisville. This plan was supported by both
political parties but opposed by labor; the plan estimated to cost
$7 million was not adopted. . . .

Several conclusions are obvious:

1. The greatest activity is in the more highly industrialized
states—California, Connecticut, Illinois, New Jersey, and New
York.

2. Many of the proposals are of the "crack-pot" variety and
had little or no hope of passage when introduced.

3. Many are aimed at refining or extending existing programs and in some cases reflect the pressure of rises in the cost
of living—unemployment compensation and public assistance.

4. In terms of quantitative effort (not too reliable an index), the greatest activity lies in public assistance, unemployment compensation, and public housing—in that order. It would appear, however, that public health and medical care constitute the leading problem, with welfare and housing ranking next.

5. Federal leadership is of signal importance in every area. Even in the *Miscellaneous* column, the proposed Merrimack Valley Authorities in New Hampshire have been labeled "a New Hampshire TVA," some of the housing bills anticipated federal action in that field, and the Hill-Burton Act certainly stimulated state activity in the hospital field.

6. A few states have assumed leadership in such areas as cash sickness benefits, and a few parallel the Federal Government in consideration of compulsory health insurance.

7. The survey was not intended to be definitive and hence did not cover every area that might be included in the term "welfare state." For example, in the civil rights field, several states have adopted comprehensive civil rights laws which supplement or parallel in part the proposed federal civil rights legislation.

This survey plus any review of recent and long-range developments would seem to support the belief that great pressures exist in favor of the development and extension of the welfare state in America. The internal improvements policy of John Quincy Adams and Henry Clay, the development of regulatory agencies in the late nineteenth century, the Square Deal of Theodore Roosevelt, the New Freedom of Woodrow Wilson, the New Deal of Franklin Roosevelt—are some of the historical precedents. Each of them represented nationalizing influences and hence changed the character of our federal system—but none of them carried the great economic and political implications of the present trend. . . .

It is pertinent to raise these questions:

a. Are we not tending to nationalize such services as health, education, and housing?

b. Is such nationalization of services a prelude to the socialization of the economy?

c. Is such nationalization of services compatible with our federal system?

There can be no doubt that there is a great nationalizing movement underway and that health, education, and housing are current examples—but merely forerunners of a far-reaching development which may ultimately embrace a full service structure.

THE GENERAL WELFARE CLAUSE [5]

In a recent radio address President Truman criticized . . . [his] critics and said, "They are just about a hundred and sixty years behind the times because the preamble to the United States Constitution states specifically that the government was established 'to promote the general welfare'." . . .

It is . . . important to reexamine the "general welfare" clause carefully to see whether it actually grants the broad powers claimed for it.

It is true the preamble states that one purpose of the Constitution is to "promote the general welfare." But this statement is not a delegation of power. The "general welfare clause" that delegates power is in Section 8 of Article I, which enumerates the powers of Congress. Clause I of this section, in defining the taxing power of Congress says, "The Congress shall have power to lay and collect taxes, duties, imposts and excises, to pay the debts and provide for the common defence and general welfare of the United States."

The interpretation to be placed on the phrase "general welfare of the United States" poses a large question. [Justice Joseph] Story, writing in 1833 about this clause said, "It has been in the past time, it is at the present time, and it will probably in all future time, continue to be the debatable ground of the Constitution. . . . Here the advocates of state rights and the friends of the Union will meet in hostile array. And here those

[5] From an article by Karl B. Lutz, Pittsburgh attorney. *American Bar Association Journal.* 36:196-8. March 1950. Reprinted by permission. The portion of Mr. Lutz's article reprinted here gives the legal background of the controversial "general welfare" clause of the Constitution. In portions not presented here, Mr. Lutz argues that through a broad interpretation of the clause, "The wide opportunity . . . opened for national control and regulation of the individual citizens and for growth of a strong, all-powerful central government must disturb every believer in the American federal system."

who have lost power will maintain long and arduous struggles
to regain the public confidence, and those who have secured
power will dispute every position which may be assumed for attack, either of their policy or their principles."

In 1892 the United States Supreme Court said, "It would be
difficult to suggest a question of larger importance, or one the
decision of which would be more far reaching." Today it is
even more evident that the general welfare clause is an important battleground in the fight for the preservation of our federal
system. . . .

In construing language of the United States Constitution
reference is seldom made to the Articles of Confederation, because of certain basic differences in the two forms of government. Yet, where language of the Constitution was obviously
carried over from the Articles, considerable information may be
gained from a study of its meaning in the Articles.

The phrase "general welfare" occurs twice in the Articles,
the phrase "general interests" occurs once, and the word "welfare" occurs once. Under the Articles, Congress had no powers
other than those definitely delegated to it, and certainly could
not have advanced the "general welfare" indirectly by acting
directly on the individual citizens within the states. The context shows that in each case the language quoted was referring
to the welfare of the confederation taken as an entire unit in
relation to its external affairs.

More specifically, Article VIII of the Articles commences
with this language:

All charges of war, and all other expenses that shall be in-
curred for the common defense or general welfare . . . shall be
defrayed out of a common treasury [supplied by requisition on
the states].

Comparing this clause with the common defense and general
welfare clause of the Constitution, Story points out that the
"objects or purposes" to which the money is to be applied are
the same, the only difference being the method of raising the
money; under the Articles by requisition, under the Constitution
by taxes.

Reports of the proceedings in the Constitutional Convention lead to the conclusion that when the phrases "general welfare" or "general interests" were used in debate, the context pointed to the external interests of the Union as a whole, contrasted with the internal interests of the individual states. It is no wonder therefore that when the phrase "general welfare" was added as a limitation on the taxing power of Congress, there was no debate as to the meaning of the phrase.

In fact, Madison, in explaining why this power was not more specifically limited, said, "the omission is accounted for by an inattention to the phraseology, occasioned, doubtless, by identity with the harmless character attached to it in the instrument from which it was borrowed. . . . That the terms in question were not suspected in the convention which formed the Constitution of any such meaning as has been constructively applied to them, may be pronounced with entire confidence." The facts, as they are now known, seem to fully support Madison's statement.

The first two objects for which Congress can lay taxes are:

1. The debts of a certain unit (the United States taken as a whole).

2. The common defense of a certain unit (the United States taken as a whole).

Why then, is it not logical to say that the third object is the general welfare of the United States taken as a unit, meaning its external affairs? Such a construction seems to be more plausible and consistent with the history of the Constitution and the federal system than other constructions that have been advocated.

Due to the fact that the phrase "general welfare," if not limited by history or context, is capable of very broad meanings, a wide difference of opinion soon arose as to its proper construction in the welfare clause. Those who placed emphasis on state rights and local self-government argued for a restricted meaning. Those who favored a strong central government argued for a broad interpretation.

Madison and Jefferson took the view that "general welfare" was a mere heading for the enumerated powers that follow.

This view, which would make the phrase a surplusage, has been generally rejected.

Hamilton, with his fervent desire for a strong central government, took the view that it authorized taxes for any purpose which was not purely local.

Marshall expressed the opinion that the tax power of Congress is broad, but that "Congress is not empowered to tax for those purposes which are within the exclusive province of the state."

Story discussed the subject at great length, stating in full all views that had previously been expressed, and adopting the Hamiltonian broad interpretation.

Hamilton, Marshall and Story naturally drew all the power possible from the general welfare clause, as they were seeking nourishment to build the infant national government into a central power strong enough to hold together the husky and sometimes perverse state governments.

Early in our history there arose a practical question as to whether Congress has power to finance internal improvements such as road and canals. Jefferson recommended a program of such improvements, but believed that a constitutional amendment was required, "because the objects now recommended are not among those enumerated in the Constitution, and to which it permits the public moneys to be applied." Madison and Monroe took the same view during their terms in the presidential office.

Calhoun took the opposite view. He said that popular demand for internal improvements furnished "better evidence of the true interpretation of the Constitution than the most refined and subtle arguments."

The resulting impasse between Congress and the President produced a compromise by which Congress gave grants-in-aid to the states for these improvements.

Subsequent events are summed up by the United States Supreme Court in this language:

As an examination of the acts of Congress will disclose, a large number of statutes appropriating or involving the expenditure of moneys for non-federal purposes have been enacted and carried into effect.

The opinion goes on to point out that such exp
not been challenged because no remedy was o
their constitutionality in the courts. A private
standing in court because his financial interes
money is said to be too small.

Recent proposals have been made for spending
money for aid to housing, to education and to other strictly
internal objects. As in most expenditures of federal funds, the
aims of these proposals can be made to appear as compelling
national objectives, but they seem to properly belong in the
category of "non-federal purposes."

In recent years Congress has passed laws which go beyond
merely spending tax money for purposes alleged to be within
the welfare clause. It has coupled taxation with social regulation of individual citizens. It has set up a multiplicity of national corporations which have tremendously expanded the power
of the national government.

One of these laws, the Agricultural Adjustment Act of 1933,
came before the Supreme Court in *United States* v. *Butler*. This
was the first time the general welfare clause received full consideration by the Court. After paying some attention to the
early conflict of views, the Court held the act invalid because
it was not merely an appropriation in aid of agriculture. "It
invades the reserved rights of the states. It is a statutory plan
to regulate and control agricultural production, a matter beyond
the powers delegated to the Federal Government."

A year later the Social Security Act came before an altered
Supreme Court in *Helvering* v. *Davis*, and was upheld as a valid
use of the power given Congress to tax for the general welfare.
The Court adopted the full Hamiltonian view, and said that
Congress is the sole judge of what constitutes the general
welfare.

The position taken by the Court in *Helvering* v. *Davis*
amounts to saying that anything that improves the lot of some
of the citizens is a valid exercise of the general welfare clause,
as long as it operates over the entire country. . . .

The interpretation suggested herein, namely that the general
welfare clause relates only to the external affairs of the national

government, offers a middle ground. It avoids the Madisonian extreme of making the clause meaningless, and it gives the national government a useful power. It would authorize such national action as the purchase and annexation of additional territory, the leasing of military bases in foreign territory, and co-operation with international organizations. . . .

Exponents of social control will doubtless object that this interpretation leaves the national government with insufficient power to cope with modern conditions. The obvious answer is that if this is true, they should seek to obtain suitable amendments to the Constitution. Such is the American way. The practice of maintaining old forms of government while evading their true intent has led to unfortunate results in other countries.

ON THE WAY TO CENTRALIZATION [6]

In the loose terminology of American political debate, the term "welfare state" has no hard and fast meaning. Like the terms "rugged individualism" or "socialism" or "communism," it is variously employed, depending on one's point of view, to describe a condition either of paradise or hell on earth. . . .

As the mentors of the Fair Deal *point* out, the word "welfare" first turns up in the preamble to the Constitution, where it is explicity stated that our Constitution is established "to promote the general welfare." Today this is taken to mean that a state can best promote the general welfare by concentrating more and more power at a central point and setting up there the bureaucratic machinery necessary to get things done. The state then considers itself responsible for the material security of every citizen "from the cradle to the grave." In taking on this responsibility, the state extends the power and authority of the Federal Government, gradually moving toward what is called "statism." This, too, is such a loose term that even President Truman not long ago said that he knew of no good definition for it. We would subscribe in general to this standard definition: "Statism

[6] From "The Welfare State" and "The Fair Deal," statements of principle by the editors. *Commonweal.* 51:475-6, 643-4. February 10 and March 31, 1950. Reprinted by permission.

is the concentration of all economic controls and economic p
ning in the hands of a highly centralized government." O
viously, we have not yet gone that far in this country. But we
are on the way.

Is this centralization a good or a bad thing? There is no
pat, doctrinaire answer to that question, but before making any
reply to it, one is led first to ask another question: How much
should the state do for its citizens? Perhaps the most basic duty
of the state toward all citizens is the preservation of order, the
maintenance of security against invasion from without and violence from within. The purpose of this protection is to assure
the individual that he shall be secure and free to exercise his
personal rights and to develop as a person in as unhindered a
way as possible. Another duty of the state is to establish such
material conditions that its citizens are free from want, that they
are adequately fed, housed and clothed. Finally, a third duty of
the state is to provide for man's social well-being; since he is
not born to live or die alone, the citizen is entitled to a healthy
community life and he has, consequently, a right to expect the
state to preserve the moral good of the community.

For some time now the tendency has been for the state to
fulfill these duties to its citizens by passing protective and welfare legislation of a broad, inclusive kind. This development
has been slow in reaching the United States. From its beginnings, when Bismarck pushed the first social legislation through
the German Reichstag,[7] welfare statism became popular in Europe and subsequently took almost full form in New Zealand,
Australia and Britain; in a corrupted form it is also the social
pattern in all totalitarian states. As this historical movement indicates, the centralized state, in one form or another, has come
along in the wake of the industrial revolution to serve as a workable means sometimes to marshal the new material forces industrialism gave us and sometimes to level out the inequalities industrialism left us. With the massing of populations in cities,
with the rise of a vast proletariat class dependent on factory employment and having no productive property of its own, while
living insecurely at the mercy of business cycle fluctuations in a

---

[7] See S. B. Fay's "Bismarck's Welfare State," in section on The Welfare
State Abroad.

my, and with the tighter concentration of
ig functions in the hands of the few, it was
ole environment man now lived in had some-
led and managed by a political institution big
th this industrial way of life. The state grew
enslave or to liberate its citizens, depending on
ice it had. In any event, the state took charge,
_____ _____ _rity he needed and in the bargain he sacrificed
to it some, and occasionally nearly all, of his freedoms.

In this country the New Deal took charge in the national
emergency of 1932. It legislated a series of welfare measures
which continue to expand now under the Fair Deal: social security, federal housing, unemployment relief, minimum wage,
price supports and subsidies, anti-trust and securities regulations,
rural and river development projects. These measures, which
worked so well to put the country back on its feet in 1933, have
by and large won the support of the people. Still, Americans
remain suspicious of too much government in Washington and
so the question remains: How much more should there be? . . .

[We have] tried to follow two principles. They are as follows: "Whenever the welfare of a community requires a common action, the unity of that common action must be assured by
the higher organs of the community." And, "Whenever a task
can be satisfactorily achieved by the initiative of the individual
or that of small social units, the fulfillment of that task must be
left to the initiative of the individual or to that of the small social units." Now these principles hardly provide one with sufficient reason for either wholesale condemnation or unqualified
praise of the welfare state and all its works. On the basis of
these principles, we have supported it at times, opposed it at
others. In every case we have been reluctant to see the individual surrender his initiative to the state, unless it has been clearly
necessary for the common good, since we believe that the
strength and the vitality of a free society depend directly and
ultimately on how free the person is to think, to talk, to make
decisions for himself, and to worship as he sees fit. The vitality
of a free society does not come from the fiat of a ruling group
at the top.

We do not look on the welfare state as inevitably trampling personal initiative to death, or as an evil in itself. But we do believe that it is potentially a serious threat to a free society, to the liberal tradition of personal independence. If the present welfare state can be seen as still evolving, still developing its techniques, we are hopeful that eventually it will pass through the centralizing stage it is now in and will gradually work toward decentralization of which there are already signs in Britain, giving the individual a more personal sense of sharing in the management of his affairs, as, for example, through such techniques as local cooperative enterprises. In the last analysis, every advance of the welfare state must be watched and judged principally on two counts: does it threaten essential personal liberties, and how does it affect the moral vitality of a community of free persons? . . .

Although President Truman has not explicitly defined the term "Fair Deal," he has made its meaning clear in applying the phrase to his legislative program; this program, as a policy of economic and civil democracy, is what he feels the Federal Government should enact to insure the welfare and security of the citizen and the state. What he proposes is, in part, a continuation of the Roosevelt New Deal and, in part, an extension of the New Deal philosophy.

Since Mr. Truman's program is in some respects related in purpose and technique to Socialist doctrine and to the Socialist ideal of "fair shares for all," the Fair Deal is frequently spoken of as leading to socialism and to state ownership of productive wealth. Actually such a development would be contrary to the intentions of the Fair Deal. Whether or not one looks on socialism as a desirable end, it is well, especially in the normally emotional atmosphere of politics, to distinguish between welfare statism, which is nearly universal today, and socialism itself; while the possibility of socialism is not remote, there appears to be no inexorable law according to which a welfare state must become a Socialist state. What, in fact, are the President's principal proposals and in what direction do they seem to be taking us?

Among the Fair Deal measures are some, such as federal aid for housing, extension of social security to cover certain occupations not covered now, and additional river valley and regional projects, all of which are meant to carry on already successful New Deal experiments and bring them up to date. Experience has shown that these are matters that the Federal Government, rather than private or local agencies, can most efficiently and economically handle. The Administration's labor policy, also fundamentally in the spirit of the New Deal reforms, has been principally a crusade to repeal the Taft-Hartley Law; in this the Administration has taken a somewhat negative view of present labor-management relations in proposing a virtual return to the Wagner Act, before writing a more satisfactory national labor law.

Among the measures which may be considered rather broad extensions of the New Deal are federal aid for public education, strong fair employment practices and civil rights legislation, increased federal pensions, national medical insurance and the Brannan farm plan. . . . Although the Administration's plan to provide old age security is not yet fully worked out, there are tentative proposals for the Federal Government to pay a pension of $100 or more a month to everyone over 65. . . . The national medical insurance plan . . . would be financed through a compulsory 3 per cent tax on all payrolls, employer and empoyee contributing equally. In receiving his fee, the doctor could choose a straight salary, or the payment of a fixed sum per patient or per visit of the patient to his office, or a combination of these methods. Although the plan calls for local administration, the Federal Government would ultimately pay the doctor bill and support the bureaucracy necessary to handle the financial and clerical paper work in an operation of this size. . . .

The Brannan plan is the Administration's proposal to reduce the country's huge and growing pile of farm surpluses and lower the price of food at the same time. In allowing certain foods to find their own price levels on a free market, rather than pegging the prices at parity levels, the Brannan plan, with its lower prices, would appeal to the consumer. It would attract the farmer simultaneously by paying him the difference between what he receives for his products on the free market and what he would have received at the parity, or supported, price level. No one can say what all these subsidies and the additional administrative personnel would cost the Federal Government and no one can say that the plan would reduce surpluses and food prices. . . .

In its regard for the welfare and security of the nation, the Fair Deal has, then, increased the power and functions of the Federal Government but not, we believe, to the extent of undermining the American ideal of personal freedom. On the whole, the effect of the Fair Deal measures reviewed here will be to distribute the national wealth and to equalize economic and political rights. There is in the Truman Administration a drift toward centralization, as there is in most modern governments, and we believe that one cannot be unconcerned about this, since it can, unless checked, make us a country of political dependents without initiative and it can, finally, take us to totalitarianism. At this time there is in the free world, wherever welfare statism or socialism have been practiced, a disillusionment with topheavy central governments, but not with the welfare benefits these governments have provided. If now there is a movement toward decentralization, and a greater reliance on the will of the individual to manage these benefits and his own affairs through local and cooperative practices, there is reason to believe that democratic governments, among them the Fair Deal, can save themselves and the personal freedoms they live by.

RECOGNIZING "SOCIALISM" [8]

Socialism, by dictionary definition, may be called a theory aiming at public collective ownership of land and capital, and the public collective management of all industry.

That sounds pretty bad, but note we call it a "dictionary definition." For there are right-wing, center and left-wing Socialists, just as in any other political movement. Left-wingers may tend to complete collectivism, as complete as the Communist theory which would divide *all* things, including the profits of individual labor, among members of the community.

[8] From "Socialism, Monster or Neighbor?" by Joseph W. LaBine, public opinion expert. *Kiwanis Magazine*. 35:5-6. April 1950. Reprinted by permission.

Right-wing Socialists, on the other hand, are those who would claim for public collective ownership only those natural resources and utilities which, they believe, can be operated in the greater public interest by government itself. . . .

A strong case can be built for the argument that America, while on the one hand lambasting socialism, has to a certain extent accepted it. That case, in fact, has already been built in public opinion surveys conducted a few months ago by the Psychological Corporation, a New York research organization.

One thousand average adults were asked a simple question: Are you for or against socialism in this country? And, as might be expected, 75.3 per cent said they were against it. Only 6.3 per cent favored it and the remaining 18.4 per cent answered with admirable candor that they simply didn't know.

We can dismiss, for present purposes, all but that 75.3 per cent who answered forthrightly that they oppose socialism. The Psychological Corporation went back and questioned this group again, coming up with a puzzling discovery: These people oppose socialism in the abstract, sure enough, yet a lot of them actually favor many socialistic measures!

Almost two thirds of them, for example, endorse the minimum wage law whereby the government sets a wage below which no interstate business can pay—yet 38 per cent of them brand it socialistic.

Three fourths of them support payroll taxes, deductions from a person's salary to produce old age, unemployment and other benefits. Is it socialistic? An emphatic yes from 27 per cent of these people!

How about the Tennessee Valley Authority and other government-owned flood control and electrical power projects? Again, two thirds of them favor it, even though 37 per cent of them say it's socialistic.

And what do they think of government-built apartment houses rented to low-income people at less than cost? It's a good idea, say 59 per cent of them. Socialistic? Yes, say 46 per cent!

That isn't all. The rent control law is approved by 43 per cent of them, but it's pure and simple socialism in the minds of

one half. Food subsidies on farm products? About one quarter
of them endorse this idea, but 55 per cent call it socialism.

The Psychological Corporation draws an obvious but interesting inference from this shocking evidence of muddled American
thinking—namely that socialism as a word or symbol, and socialism in terms of specific steps in government control, are
clearly two different things. Three quarters of us fear the symbol, but we don't translate it into a fear of specific socialistic
measures.

Socialism, in short, has become a "scare word," and unfortunately so because we cannot think rationally and calmly about
anything we are afraid of. . . .

Perhaps we in America may come to accept certain socialistic
measures; certainly, for better or for worse, the trend toward
human-welfare legislation has quickened impressively [in] the
past two decades.

Whatever happens, though, socialism would in itself be the
secondary danger, so long as it represented the intelligently expressed will of the people. The real peril is that we may
blunder into socialism unintentionally, without knowing where
we are going!

RAISING THE BASIC QUESTIONS [9]

[To begin its examination of the welfare state, one group of
college students at *Mademoiselle's* forum,] headed by Arthur N.
Holcombe, professor of government at Harvard, went right back
to basics to formulate a definition of the welfare state in its application to our own American system. They went back to the
definition offered first by public-opinion analyst Elmo Roper:
A state which attacks systematically the five basic hazards of
modern life—disease, ignorance, squalor, idleness and want—by
government action.

Government action against disease isn't a new idea, as Mr.
Holcombe demonstrated in his historical review of welfare meas-

[9] From "The Welfare State in a Free Society." *Mademoiselle.* 31:226-9+.
August, 1950. Reprinted by permission. This article is a report on *Mademoiselle's*
Seventh College Forum, attended by fifty-eight college students, and held in
New York, April 15, 1950.

ures in the United States. The first step, long ago, was the establishment of the Marine Hospital Service; this grew into the Quarantine Service and recently into the Federal Public Health Service. As far back as 1787 we began to make provisions for public education. Mr. Roper had shown that the attack on idleness (lack of steady jobs) and want is not a new thing in the Western world. In England and Germany in the last century the beginnings of what we now call a social security program were developing. Even the poor law acts enacted in England in the seventeenth century might be cited as early "welfare statism." The welfare state, Mr. Roper went on, is perfectly compatible with any of the three kinds of economy prevalent today —the police state, where all forms of human activity are closely regulated by the state; democratic socialism, where individual freedom and political rights are guaranteed but economic responsibility is taken by the state; and a capitalistic democracy such as we have, where the state does not assume the responsibility either for the economic or for the political part of life. The welfare state is not a fourth system in itself.

The group compared this with Mr. Holcombe's definition of a welfare state as one where special emphasis is placed on the use of the welfare power, "the power to promote the public interest by spending public money for the benefit of particular persons or classes of persons or by putting public property at the service of such persons."

Mr. Holcombe . . . gave five illustrations of fields in which govvernment action might conceivably be considered in the public interest—religion, education, health, development of national resources and development of transportation and communication. He pointed out that the first—religion—was certainly considered basic to the welfare of the people by early Americans. But because religious tolerance was a cardinal principle in our democracy, this area was expressly forbidden in the Constitution. In all the other fields, Congress has used the welfare power as and when it saw fit, in accordance with growing needs and changing ideas of government responsibility. One of the first steps in the development of national resources was the homestead policy, by which land was given away to those who would settle on it and make it productive. It was denounced as socialistic and communistic by many at the time. Today the development of atomic energy is a center of controversy, with government forced to maintain a strong control and some people believing that the free enterprise system is threatened thereby. So the welfare power, which was written into our Constitution at its beginning, has always been used and is now being used more and more.

Mildred Kiefer of Columbia asked Mr. Holcombe if he thought full employment was one of the functions of the welfare state and if so, whether or not there was a historical background for it. Mr. Holcombe felt that full employment was one of the functions of government if the people, speaking through their representatives, thought so; and that the record of the past establishes a precedent for "practically anything that the Congress might see fit to do."

But Mr. Holcombe drew a sharp distinction between our government and a real welfare state. The proposed budget for the next fiscal year, he said, includes over $29 billion for war purposes compared to over $9 billion for all other purposes, including welfare—a ratio of more than three to one. "It seems to me that we have primarily a military state and a welfare state only secondarily."

The students came to the general conclusion that the welfare state is susceptible of several varying though not necessarily conflicting definitions; and that in this country we have something which could more accurately be called an increasing measure of welfare statism rather than a real, functioning welfare state. As Mr. Holcombe said, "We have gone a considerable distance on the path toward fulfillment of the implications of the preamble of the Constitution, but we still have a long distance to go." He believes that the government, without any formal amendment of the Constitution, may become a welfare state if Congress should decide that such a development is necessary and proper.

Now the discussion moved on to perhaps the crucial question of the whole day: Is the welfare state a good thing or is it not? What are its drawbacks and its advantages? The difficulties in attaining it or in retreating from it?

The purpose of this kind of state, the students decided, is to find a reasonable balance between progress and security. In this they had the strong backing of Elmo Roper who, as research director of the Fortune Surveys of Public Opinion, has a wide base for judgment. The American people, he stated, want—and believe they can have—security, freedom *and* economic opportunity. "They want the chance to improve their economic lot under free enterprise; they also want to be protected against the hazards of that system; and finally they want their personal liberties and political freedom kept intact and not compromised one iota."

Rosemary Beeching, of Barnard, wondered if people had not changed their ideas of what freedoms are most important, as they have their ideas of welfare. She asked Mr. Roper if his surveys showed that individual freedoms were no longer as important as the new economic freedoms. Mr. Roper's reply was that freedoms may seem to become less important because they are taken for granted—for example, the number-one freedom wanted by Europeans in a recent survey was the freedom not to have their homes invaded by the police. That was never mentioned by Americans. Following this up, Jeanette Sarkisian of Northwestern said she thought the new emphasis on economic freedom might stem from the fact that the people are much more conscious that their way of life doesn't offer the security they had been led to believe. Insecurity, she argued, is much more immediately threatening than the hydrogen bomb. Mr. Roper agreed, and remarked that people may be willing in some cases to give up a little freedom for security, or to modify what had once been regarded as freedom.

The question as Mr. Roper posed it was: Is this wish for security plus freedom plus economic opportunity "a mirage of merely trying to have our cake and eat it too or is it a realization of the democratic dream on a level never thought of before?"

While the discussion was going on, another group . . . was delving deeper into the same problem—is the welfare state good or bad? And can we have it, in any case? Paul Porter, whose career reads like a government directory—from Agricultural Ad-

justment Administration to Office of Economic Stabilization—
emcee'd this session. . . .

Mr. Porter's group was disturbed by the inefficiency of
"bureaucracy," the possibility of making bad mistakes in expanding a welfare program. The students remembered, and
quoted, the question which [Republican Oren] Root had posed
squarely: Are the people of this country willing to find their
security through their own efforts, or will they hand over their
power of decision

to a distant and all-powerful Federal Government? . . . There will
always be enough seekers after power to reach out and grab the
decision-making from the hands of the people. . . . If the people delegate
to the central government great welfare powers only when they are
necessary because the individual and local governments are not in a
position to act, then I think the welfare state will be kept within reasonable bounds and we have no need to fear our freedom. . . . If the people
want bread and circuses, I think they will get bread and circuses. . . .

How much government action can we stand before the control
of our economic life rests in the hands of public officialdom and
not upon the decisions of private owners and managers of free
enterprise? Many of the girls agreed with Mr. Roper's answer,
which was the middle answer—that it is the job of government
to guarantee protection against the hazards of economic fluctua-
tion. This doesn't mean that government will determine the
direction of the economy, but that it will be a buffer against
cyclical insecurity. According to the middle view, this is the
social cost of keeping the channels of private initiative and enterprise open.

Barbara Leh of Stanford challenged Mr. Roper's point of
view. "Wouldn't there always be an excuse for government
regulation? . . . Would it be just a temporary aid in times of
stress? Wouldn't we always be in times of stress?" That some
of the so-called stopgap legislation will become (as some already
has) a permanent part of our system, Mr. Roper agreed. (He
mentioned one of his New England ancestors in the late 1600s,
who was expelled from the board of selectmen for "advocating
the seditious and heretic policy of free public education.") On
the other side, Mr. Porter cited the liquidation of controls in the

OPA, of which he was once administrator; and the provisions in the federal rent control statute that whenever the individual states want to assume this responsibility the Federal Government will relinquish it.

Margaret Wedel of Stephens wondered if the government, because of its power and its unlimited resources, wouldn't be in a position to stifle private enterprise entirely if it entered into competition. Mr. Porter felt that the wartime record of the government in controlling prices and production only as necessary and in relinquishing controls as soon as it became feasible, proved that possibility an imaginary one. He cited the Tennessee Valley Authority, whose head Gordon Clapp, was one of the day's speakers. He reminded the girls of what Mr. Clapp had said: that more "pilot projects" like the TVA might be very valuable in "needling" private business to do more. The TVA, Mr. Clapp had explained, generates almost all the electricity in its region; but because the local communities own and operate the distribution, there is a restraining influence which prevents it from growing too powerful.

The argument over government in industry wound up at Mr. Clapp's illustration of the electrical industry. There have been more and more demands for cooperative or government operations that will take electricity into rural areas where the private companies won't go. If industry can't attract capital to spread service to less profitable areas, Mr. Clapp said, government will. But if, for instance, steel produces fully, we won't be operating steel plants under government auspices, "and the steel industries know that. The threat to do so may be a very good stimulant."

The delegates then took up in detail the Republican argument presented by Mr. Root, who as one of the young, liberal leaders of the Republican party, agreed that the welfare of the people was a commendable aim but believed that the centralization of power in Washington was the wrong way to go about it. The Republican view is that all problems are best solved at the closest possible level to the people. By individuals whenever possible; if that fails then by local government, then state, and by the Federal Government only as a last resort. President Truman's threat, that the government might build and operate steel plants if steel production did not rise covered an area in which, according to Mr. Root, government should in no event intercede. Mr. Porter, in his answer, argued that the steel companies are trying to maintain a price level by curtailing production. Since steel is one of the important bases of our economy, he believes it is the function of government to step in if the industrial system, by its own operation, cannot fill the need.

Mr. Root recommended that in some cases government should function in assistance to individuals—as in the Republican health bill. Unlike the Democratic bill, it calls for an expansion and development of existing private insurance agencies with standards to be set and financial aid given by government. (Mr. Porter's comment on this: "If the Federal Government can prevent hoof and mouth disease in animals, certainly it can do no less for human beings.")

Mr. Root said that there were times when government should accept primary responsibility but allow individuals to share in the operation of the plan—for instance, the New York state disability insurance. The government requires payroll deduction, but the insurance itself is handled competitively by both the state-owned insurance fund and private insurance companies. Then there are times when the government must take full responsibility. But these matters are often better handled by the state—for instance, rent control. The Federal Government can and should function only where all else fails, for example in labor and management relations in interstate commerce. (Mr. Porter complained that Mr. Root seemed to want the Federal Government to be a kind of receiver for all the unsolved and unresolved problems which the local communities and the states could not handle.)

One of the girls brought up the point that there would be just as much power-seeking and profit-seeking among private companies handling welfare measures as there would be in the government. Mr. Root agreed, but maintained that when people assume responsibility for their own welfare as much as possible, there is more of a sense of participation which is a healthy check on any power-seekers.

Mr. Porter, in answering Mr. Root's preference for having local government handle welfare measures, maintained that we live in a society so interrelated that our problems can no longer be attacked and solved on a local basis. Mr. Holcombe had touched on another facet of the same problem in answer to a question by Helen Schimmenti of Wheaton about whether the states, by starting such things as a health program, might help to break the ground for federal legislation. Mr. Holcombe answered that it would; but the development of the tax law has given the Federal Government access to such enormous revenue and has limited that of the states to such a degree that it often isn't possible to start an expensive program on the state level. . . .

After the centralization of power, Mr. Root's next major objection to the welfare state was that it is fiscally unsound. This divided the group along straight Republican and Democratic lines. Mr. Root's simple proposition was that the general welfare is not promoted by any course which leads to an unbalanced budget—that a $5 billion deficit in peacetime, in the greatest prosperity mankind has ever known, cannot possibly contribute to the general welfare. Mr. Porter's equally simple answer was that the Eightieth Republican-controlled Congress repealed the tax proposals which would have achieved a balanced budget.

Dorothy Orr, of the University of Oregon, quoted Senator John McClelland, who asked where the money was going to come from, "If we do not stop passing laws calling for more and more spending there is neither prospect nor hope for revenues to cover and again overtake or equal expenditures." Mr. Porter answered that he could conceive of these welfare measures developing so that the tax level could be less than it is now—for instance, a self liquidating health plan or power development. He agreed that a balanced budget is desirable, but pointed out that with sixty-five or seventy cents of every dollar going for military purposes this was hardly possible. The ultimate of a welfare state is not the complete concentration of money within the central government, he said, nor the making of every decision from the central government in Washington.

On this subject Helen Miller of Wellesley asked if there might not be a political revulsion as deficits accumulated; Mr. Porter replied that we now have many times what we first thought of as an unmanageable national debt, but that we are nevertheless getting a magnificent operation from our industrial system. Policies to expand production and increase the total amount of goods will eventually change our ideas of national income to the trillions rather than the billions, he believes.

The discussion ended with the conclusion expressed by so many of the speakers: the inevitability of increasing welfare measures in our society. As Mr. Clapp had said about government in the electrical industry, "Whether that is good or bad seems irrelevant. That is what will happen."

MERITS OF THE WELFARE STATE

A LONG-RANGE AMERICAN DEVELOPMENT [1]

Perhaps the best brief description of the New Deal is the term "welfare state." Beginning in 1933 the state has openly, and as a normal rather than an exceptional policy, taken the responsibility for the welfare of the mass of the American people —for social security, working conditions, farming, conservation and, less aggressively, for housing, civil rights, health and education. It has taken this responsibility not only by standing between the individual and disaster but in the more positive fashion of protecting and advancing his prosperity and happiness.

Though it is common to regard the welfare state as an invention—or a borrowing—of Franklin Roosevelt and to describe it as a foreign importation, or a Communist plot, it is, in fact, older than, let us say, the doctrine of "liberty of contract," long celebrated by rugged individualists, and more native than the doctrine of laissez-faire, whose very name advertises its foreign origin. The beginnings of the welfare state may be traced back at least to the decades of the 1880s and 1890s, . . . to the rise of modern industry and capitalism and urban life in the United States. . . .

In the beginning the government—first state, then federal— addressed itself to regulation rather than to control or to creation. This function of government is now so widely accepted that it seems almost irrelevant to mention it; yet in its day such things as federal supervision of railroads, the income tax, conservation and agricultural relief were denounced as subversive, socialistic and communistic, and federal centralization was held destructive of the foundations of the republic. Indeed, the trumpets and alarms over centralization sounded a good deal earlier in our history:

[1] From "Appraisal of the Welfare State," by Henry Steele Commager, professor of history, Columbia University. New York *Times Magazine*. p10+. May 15, 1949. Reprinted by permission.

The government [we read] has been fundamentally altered . . .
instead of confining itself in time of peace to the diplomatic and commercial relations of the country, it is seeking out employment for itself
by interfering in the domestic concerns of society, and threatens in the
course of a very few years to control in the most offensive and despotic
manner all the pursuits, the interests, the opinions and the conduct of
men.

Thus Hugh Legaré—at one time Secretary of State—writing
in 1828.

What, then, are some of the antecedents of the welfare state?
First, perhaps, the program of internal improvements which
President John Quincy Adams (it was against him that Legaré
directed his diatribe) wanted to make the cornerstone of his
presidential policy. A titanic debate raged, for over half a century, over his program; who now recalls it but the historian, or
who questions the propriety of federal action in this arena?

A second major antecedent of the welfare state is the land
grant and homestead policy of the government formulated in
the 1850s and launched during the Civil War. The Federal Government subsidized the construction of western railroads to the
tune of about 180 million acres of public land, while states added
additional tens of millions. At the same time the Homestead Act
of 1862, and subsequent land acts, gave over 200 million acres
of public lands to farmers, ranchers, and timbermen. It was, in a
sense, a relief program; it was, too, a welfare program.

A third body of antecedents came during the period when
William Graham Sumner was preaching the Spencerian gospel of
laissez-faire. But it was the period, too, when the philosophical
foundations for the welfare state were being built. Lester Ward,
greatest of American sociologists, drew the blueprints; a group
of economists and historians, including John R. Commons, Rich-
ard Ely, E. A. Ross, Simon Patten and Woodrow Wilson, proceeded to construct the edifice—construct it with the aid of
practical workingmen like the elder La Follette, Altgeld, Pingree
and Bryan.

Responding to the problems of modern industrialism state
after state legislated to regulate railroads and trusts, assist farmers
and workingmen. State action soon proved ineffectual, for local

regulation could not cope with national problems and the responsibility was inevitably transferred to the Federal Government. Whatever we may think of the speed of the process of centralization today, it is a historical fact that the Federal Government was both slow and cautious in assuming supervisory responsibility, even in those areas where the constitutional authority was clear. Thus it required a century for the national government to enact general legislation on immigration (1882), interstate business (1887), and restraint of trade (1890).

Leadership in the creation of the welfare state was the monopoly of no one party. The Populists originally took the lead, demanding, among other things, government ownership of railroads, telephone and telegraph, a graduated income tax, government-directed inflation; to these Bryan shortly added labor legislation and guarantee of bank deposits. The Republicans, under Theodore Roosevelt, translated some of the Populists demands into legislation; the Democrats, under Woodrow Wilson, carried the welfare program into new fields. And meantime such states as Wisconsin, Oregon, Kansas and Massachusetts were embarking upon experiments which foreshadowed the legislation of the New Deal years.

There was no great difference between Roosevelt's Square Deal and Wilson's New Freedom, except that Wilson more clearly formulated a philosophy to justify the new role of government and insisted upon presidential leadership in the translation of these ideas into laws. "There has been something crude and heartless and unfeeling in our haste to succeed and be great," he said, in his First Inaugural Address, as he called upon the nation to abandon laissez-faire, reform the tariff, modernize the banking and currency system, remake the industrial system, give new vitality to agriculture through "the instrumentality of science taken directly to the farm," and to embark upon a program of conservation of natural and human resources.

There can be no equality of opportunity, [he added, in words that anticipated those Franklin Roosevelt was to use again and again] if men and women and children be not shielded in their lives, their very vitality, from the consequences of great industrial and social processes which they cannot alter, control, or singly cope with. Society must see to it that it does not itself crush or weaken or damage its own constituent parts. The first duty of law is to keep sound the society it serves. Sanitary laws, pure food laws, and laws determining conditions of labor which individuals are powerless to determine for themselves are intimate parts of the very business of justice and legal efficiency.

The first Wilson Administration saw more important social and economic legislation than any administration since that of Washington—the Federal Reserve Act, the income tax, the Federal Trade Commission and the Clayton Antitrust Act, the Adamson Act, a series of acts to help the farmers. Yet it was an advance that did little more than keep up with the mounting problems of modern economy.

The modern period of the welfare state, inaugurated in 1933 —not in 1929 as some apologists for the Hoover Administration now insist—is familiar enough. Confronted by a depression which business could not surmount, the Roosevelt Administration undertook a program which was heatedly denounced by the champions of rugged individualism. But once written into the law of the land and endorsed by the courts, it came to be generally accepted. Nothing better proves that than its endorsement, in substance, by the Republican platforms of 1940, 1944 and 1948. If it can ever be said that anything is permanent in American politics, it can be said that the New Deal is permanent.

Granted that it is permanent, where is the line to be drawn between the welfare state and socialism, between a planned and a controlled economy? Granted that business can no longer remain wholly private, where is the line to be drawn between the regulation and the destruction of private enterprise?

These are valid questions. They are given immediate urgency by President Truman's proposals for the enlargement of the New Deal into the Fair Deal, and specifically by his recommendation of federal aid to education and to public health, and his suggestion that the government might find it necessary to construct its own steel plants. Are we, in fact . . . slipping into socialism? Is this program in fact . . . the program of totalitarianism?

The critics of the welfare state have only themselves to blame
if Americans refuse to be excited by these charges or be aroused
by rusty cliches and overworked shibboleths. Yet proponents of
the welfare state themselves must be concerned by any departure
from American tradition or any deviation from the logic of
governmental activity in a democracy. How do Truman's three
proposals fit—or deviate from— that tradition and that logic?

The principle and policy of state aid to education is, needless
to say, very old. Its origins go back, interestingly enough, even
before the Constitution. Jefferson's Ordinance of 1785 provided
for the use of public lands to advance education, and the Northwest Ordinance of 1787—one of the basic laws of our history—
specifically set aside certain sections in each township and certain
townships in each state for the support of public schools, and
this on the principle that "religion, morality, and knowledge,
being necessary to good government and the happiness of mankind, schools and the means of education shall forever be encouraged."

Thereafter public lands—that is originally federal lands—
were freely devoted to support of public schools and institutions
of higher education. In 1862 the Morrill Land Grant Act set
aside additional millions of acres of public lands for the support
of agricultural and industrial schools, and most of the great state
universities of the country are "land-grant" colleges. In the
1880s the Hatch Act granted public lands to establish agricultural
experiment stations. Incidental but not irrelevant to this is the
long-accepted use of federal funds for the support of such educational institutions as the Library of Congress, the Smithsonian
Institution, and the Geological Survey. To date there has been no
important instance of improper interference by the Federal Government with educational activities.

In the last decade the Federal Government has entered en-
ergetically into the field of education. The logic of this is clear
enough. Rejections from the Army on account of illiteracy ran
to some 4 per cent. Future warfare will demand trained intelligence—above all, scientific intelligence. A government which
has the responsibility of national defense, and which can conscript
all the manpower of the nation for defense, has a legitimate

interest in education. It is against the background of this over-all military situation that we can best appreciate the significance of such varying developments as the GI Bill, the program of research scholarships, the subsidizing of scientific research, and the Fulbright Bill. It is against this background, too, that we must consider the proposal to use federal funds to equalize educational opportunities and to subsidize brains.

Although the United States Public Health Service dates back to 1798, the antecedents of federal intervention in the realm of public health are more recent—as is indeed the whole concept of "public" health. The police power of the state to interfere in matters of public health has never been successfully challenged—the right to establish quarantines, to insist upon compulsory vaccination, to require health certificates for marriage—and states established boards of health as early as 1855.

The Federal Government entered tardily into the field, and almost surreptitiously. The Pure Food and Drug Act and the Meat Inspection Act of the Theodore Roosevelt Administration were early assertions of interest; so, too, the work of the Bureau of Public Health in combating malaria and yellow fever. Under the New Deal federal contributions to public health expanded—in construction of hospitals by the WPA, for example, in the health work of the CCC, in the programs of maternity aid, aid to the blind and the crippled, and to state public health agencies under the Social Security system.

As yet, however, there has been no such large-scale invasion of the health field as of the field of education. Yet the logic behind federal interest in public health is at least as convincing as that behind federal interest in education. For where illiteracy accounted for only a small percentage of rejections from the armed services, health accounted for a shockingly large percentage. In many states that percentage ran as high as one quarter or one third; in North Carolina it ran to one half. A government which has the responsibility of maintaining its armed services and which requires certain physical standards for those services, may well insist upon its obligation to raise standards of public health.

There remains the most perplexing question of all—that of government competition in the realm of production. It is one thing to assert the public interest in an enlightened citizenry and in a population that is physically fit. It is, perhaps, another thing to embark upon a program of industrial production. Here President Truman may have overstepped that intangible line which separates the welfare from the socialistic state.

Yet here, too, there are antecedents, and here some logical support. It is relevant to remember that from an early date states built turnpikes, canals and railroads. In our own day local governments have commonly entered the field of the public utilities, and public ownership and operation of water, gas, electrical, and even transportation facilities is familiar enough. And if the Federal Reserve System has not actually nationalized the banks of the nation, it has assimilated most of them to the Federal Government.

Undoubtedly, however, the most obvious peacetime precedent for governmental intervention in the field of production is the TVA. It is probably a safe generalization that government will, in the future, use the spur of competition either to prevent monopoly or to increase production in those industries intimately and indissolubly related to the national defense.

Nor is there any reason to suppose that the program of the welfare state will be confined to what has been accomplished by the New Deal and proposed by President Truman. Walter Lippmann, who can scarcely be called a Socialist, suggested some years ago as part of the agenda of liberalism:

> Large social expenditures on eugenics and on education; the conservation of the people's patrimony in the land and natural resources; . . . insurance and indemnification against the risks and losses of technological and economic change; and many other things such as providing the opportunities for recreation which would not otherwise exist in specialized and congested communities.

To health, education, and recreation will doubtless be added more vigorous support to slum clearance and housing, a positive program in the realm of civil rights, systematic development of scientific research and especially of the manifold possibilities of atomic energy, a program of conservation and internal improvements dwarfing anything as yet undertaken, and numerous other items.

Historically, what the welfare state undertakes is to give real equality of opportunity so far as that is possible, to undermine monopoly, to equalize actual burdens, to safeguard the common wealth in natural and human resources. It attempts to do this by regulating economy, by planning for economic and social development, by protecting men and women in their civil rights, by safeguarding the health and intelligence of the people.

Whatever this may be, it is not socialism. The essence of socialism is the public ownership and management of the means of production, capital, land, and property, by the state. Soviet Russia is, in large measure, a Socialist country; Britain and Scandinavia are as yet far from true socialism. By contrast the United States retains, even after two generations of public regulation, even after . . . [seventeen] years of the New Deal, an economy of private enterprise. By contrast the American program remains a conservative one, and—it is proper to add—a democratic one. We do well to remember the warning which President Roosevelt sounded in 1938:

> Democracy has disappeared in several other great nations, not because the people of those nations disliked democracy, but because they had grown tired of unemployment and insecurity. . . . In desperation they chose to sacrifice liberty in the hope of getting something to eat. We in America know that our democratic institutions can be preserved and made to work. But in order to preserve them we need . . . to prove that the practical operation of democratic government is equal to the task of protecting the security of the people.

POSITIVE ACHIEVEMENTS SINCE 1933 [2]

Few remember today the campaign of 1932; depression, idle factories, one third of the population out of work, banks, credit, currency in the worst catastrophe in American history. The American people, believing that economic life worked automatically, and that the government's chief business was to keep the peace, had accepted all this despairingly for three years as it

[2] From "Lest We Forget," by A. A. Berle, Jr., attorney and former government official. *Survey.* 85:69-71. February 1949. Reprinted by permission.

might accept an earthquake or a flood or a hurricane. Such misery in a rich and capable country was, to be sure, intolerable, unjust, irrational; but the automatic workings of uncontrolled enterprise and private initiative were relied on to bring conditions back to normal. Only—here was the rub—huge numbers of people simply had to eat. Without jobs, they could not pay for their keep. Cities, counties, and states had not money to feed them. In the course of the campaign, after grave deliberation, Roosevelt took a huge leap. He pledged that the Federal Government would become responsible for and financially assist relief!

This seems, now, like a tiny step. Then, it was daring politics—a clear-cut undertaking, by a candidate for national office, that the Federal Government would move in on economics, if economics could not put on a better act than it was doing. This was followed by other decisions introduced in campaign speeches and later embodied in the measures now known as the "New Deal." Social security; parity prices for farmers; public works and other measures to establish employment; a Reconstruction Finance Corporation equipped to keep the capital markets open; attention to youth through Civilian Conservation Camps and the National Youth Administration; balanced development of electric power and rural electrification; a huge experiment in regional planning in the Tennessee Valley; policing of the stock exchanges and utility holding companies.

The bitterness with which each of these proposals was greeted and fought in some circles is a matter of history. The battle is over now, save as a residuum of bitterness toward the personality Franklin Roosevelt remains endemic in some quarters. The measures were accepted one by one, after a series of congressional battles, as politics permitted. Crude, only partly integrated, they were all great, groping strides toward a new conception which now takes more or less permanent shape. The idea has been christened variously. It is sometimes called the "welfare state"; the *Manchester Guardian* usually refers to it as the "insurance state." But President Truman's . . . name for it is the Fair Deal.

It was this over-all conception of a socially just system which really won the election of 1948. No other analysis stands up.

More votes were cast for the Congress than for the presidency. The advocates of the conception of a state which would be socially just—men like [Democratic Senator] Paul Douglas, for instance, in Illinois—ran far ahead of their tickets. Organized labor helped—as did liberal campaigners and others. But the job was done by a ground swell of American voters. A popular plebiscite was being taken on a proposition only partly stated by the political leadership. The proposition was that in a country capable of producing and earning a national annual income of $240 billion you can have both private life and a government system that will make American economics take care of the American people through adequate production and also with a moderate approximation to horse sense and justice.

The program now appearing in President Truman's message on the [1949] State of the Union reflects the fact that John Citizen not only stated his proposition, but knew, in a general way, how he expected to get there.

Social Security was perhaps first in his thinking. The 80th Congress had cut three quarters of a million workers out of the social security system; the voters, however, wanted to include practically everybody in old age and unemployment coverage. The 80th Congress had scornfully thrown aside the idea that Social Security could likewise include health insurance; the voters wanted it. The general drift of thinking really favored a cradle-to-grave system of insurance, guaranteeing everybody who keeps ordinary faith with civilization at least subsistence. When annual national income is running at about $1400 per person, even with inflated prices you can come close to realizing the ideal.

Education, too. Historically, education is governed by localities—and still is. One result has been wide opportunity in wealthier sections of the country, and little opportunity in less favored areas. Even conservatives like Senator Taft were prepared to tackle federal aid to education. . . . Anyway, something like equality of educational opportunity was wanted. New on the political scene, it was in fact a variant of the 1938 proposal to establish a national youth service administration including aid for needy high school students and work scholarships for college students.

Less universal but closely linked with this was a strong desire in most parts of the country to wipe out certain of the more obvious racial discriminations. Resisted by the Dixiecrat states, the federal program of civil rights made a strong appeal elsewhere. There are those who remember that this is a logical evolution from Franklin Roosevelt's Fair Employment Practices Commission, and from Eleanor Roosevelt's championing the cause of human equality. . . .

Cynics insist this is merely a vote for Santa Claus. They are mistaken. Several other propositions are included, building up to the point of a balanced and planned economy. During the campaign, everybody read about private initiative, the dangers of bureaucracy, the road to serfdom via socialism and bankruptcy of the government, and so forth. A clear majority of the United States decided this sort of talk was chiefly applesauce. If they had looked a little behind the returns they might have decided that it was not even healthy applesauce. The campaign against health insurance, for instance, was carried on by a so-called "National Committee of Physicians," financed chiefly by a few drug and medicine manufacturers.

The supposedly automatic results of the law of supply and demand came in for an overhauling. The 80th Congress had thrown out price control. Charges had been widely circulated that a new OPA was equivalent to establishing a Gestapo. The average voter, and particularly his wife, thought otherwise. He, or she, knew very little about discussion of learned economists on the subjects of "administered prices" and "imperfect competition" but they grasped the central idea, namely, that large scale business, especially as it approaches monopoly, does not work on a basis of supply and demand. Prices under a concentrated corporation system do not fall easily; it is employment that drops, not prices.

People voted for a program which included extending rent controls, setting up stand-by price controls, permitting moderate credit controls, all aimed to shave the top off inflationary booms. President Roosevelt had said somewhat the same thing—in peacetime, too—when he proposed "yardsticks" as a method of keeping down power rates—and before that when he had endeavored to crystallize the conception of a "just price" in the National Recovery Administration.

The thinking of 1948 also carried forward acceptance of the idea that the government, where necessary, might enter into direct production. Political theorists argued that this was the nose of a Socialist camel entering the American tent. The public seemed unimpressed. Government had entered direct production, particularly in electricity with the building of the Boulder Dam, the Tennessee Valley project, and the Columbia River developments. Discernibly, the . . . [1948] vote endorsed the Tennessee Valley Authority, and wanted more like it including further development of power in the southwest, and in the Columbia River system, and harnessing the huge dynamo latent in the St. Lawrence River. This might be "government in business"—but not enough to impair the private enterprise system. Propagandists could and did roar; but the average individual, especially in Knoxville or the State of Washington, knew from his own experience that the Columbia, Colorado, and Tennessee developments had really provided a base on which more private enterprise was being built than ever before—both actually and proportionately. President Roosevelt had made the point years ago; and he had made the experiments, too. Huge as they were, they were nevertheless pilot plants for greater developments of needed production.

There is a strong bias, clearly, in favor of private production and private operation wherever possible. The principle, however, is that where production is needed and cannot be got on reasonable terms through private channels, the Federal Government is justified in stepping in and producing. President Truman's remark that if steel could not be got otherwise, the Federal Government should produce it, carried forward a decision which President Roosevelt had made earlier in the field of public power and in public housing. Primary reliance is on private capital and private operation to provide these basic necessities. If this method proves unable to meet the demand—well, people still need electricity and housing, and the Federal Government has the right and responsibility to move in.

The Federal Government in 1933 undertook responsibility for making the huge economic complex which is the United States keep running and keep progressing. The commentator observed then that no President could ever again limit the responsibilities and functions of the presidency as they had been limited in the administrations of Coolidge and Hoover; no American administration could say that its job was keeping peace and public order, leaving economic conditions to drift where the winds of private finance and business might drive. The conception had been wholly changed by Franklin Roosevelt; the methods will be worked out in time. Truman accepted the fact and its implications. Now, the broad outlines of ways and means are being steadily filled in; and the election of 1948 on the Truman elaboration of the Roosevelt doctrine settled the point that the responsibility assumed by FDR would not be relinquished. Nor will it—by any party—in the foreseeable future.

There are, of course, problems ahead, and they are clearly visible. President Roosevelt never did solve the task of making peacetime American economy run to full capacity or to supply sixty million jobs—except in wartime. But he was struggling to overcome the accumulated superstition and the out-dated economic doctrine of the entire nineteenth century. In the 1930s, it was seriously thought that expansion of the currency necessarily meant inflation, and that a billion-dollar deficit meant rubber dollars. The war taught us that inflation does not occur while there are idle plants and unemployed men; it occurs only when you are running at or near full capacity.

Roosevelt's measures today seem absurdly small; but one has to remember that we had to conquer a solid mass of habit, accumulated experience, and alleged expert opinion developed to guide a quite different, more or less static agricultural civilization. Meantime we had built a concentrated, huge, sensitive industrial system. We were converging on the age of electronics and atomic energy. This goes by different rules, and new values appear. We were emerging from the time in which educated men held the gold content of the dollar more important than the right of a man to have a job. Property ceased to mean farms and forges, and increasingly meant stocks, bonds, and jobs. Today, technical opinion has shifted but, far more than that, values came to be newly appraised.

There was—and is—one interesting overtone in this long political evolution which now attains a settled governmental base.

The social-economic system of the United States is challenged today, and is competing with the social and economic system propounded by Communist Russia. But the American system is not competing with a reality of Russian achievement but with the claims of the dream. It is endeavoring to meet the challenge, not of anything yet realized in any Communist state, but of what they claim can be done in some distant millennium.

If the world is in for a general social revolution, the American stands an excellent chance of meeting it by the simple process of realizing the major ideals without the bother, waste, cruelty, blood and mess of revolution.

A brilliant Washington correspondent, Ernest Lindley, in 1932 christened the New Deal as "the Roosevelt Revolution"—a prophetic name. The 80th Congress may be said to have been the counter-revolutionary attack. The election of 1948 stopped it in its tracks, and the Truman Administration now has the task of enlarging, simplifying and making more clear and coherent the main lines of social responsibility assumed.

From here out we shall be debating not the assumption of responsibility but the best way of carrying it out.

The debate, I think, will be healthier in some ways than the early passionate struggles of the 1930s. For one thing, it is now possible to survey the whole scene; to realize that a steady flow of income with unemployment insurance supplementing wages is also a measure of keeping business on an even keel; to see that increase of public power facilities can be used to pick up slack when demand for steel falls off. Credit control and a lopsided price structure are now known to be connected. The economy which could break a man irrespective of his industry, honesty, and capability would seem today to be a mistake of men, not an act of God. The central conception of social and economic planning by free people for free people is beginning to emerge. Franklin Roosevelt, tactician as he was, knew that it was politically impossible to propose an overhaul of the entire system. He therefore worked measure by measure, fighting his separate battles on specific issues.

The debate in the aggregate is clearer; for it rests more on the general conception of live values for everyone than on appeal to the special interests of farmers in the Northwest, or job hungry constituents in the various states. These special interests will always be with us. They are less likely to influence decisions where the entire picture is presented.

In result, the moral conception which Franklin Roosevelt enunciated in his successive inaugurals is now reflected in a program designed precisely to move toward realization of those ideals.

[Seventeen] . . . years a long time, as political memory goes. A time of trouble, dispute, confusion, debate. A time of trial and error. A time of peace, a time of war, a time of something else than peace. But through it appears at length a direction; the confusion was not meaningless, the debate was not sterile. The quiet, healthy, formulated line of public thinking has been obscured on the surface but turns out to have been running strong and steady. Those of us who saw the beginning know very well that this too is not the end.

PROGRAM OF THE DEMOCRATIC PARTY [3]

We [Democrats] wish to take formal notice of the charge that our party is a "welfare party." We are proud that we have measured up to the authority and duty of the government as set forth in our Constitution to promote the general welfare and we propose to continue to promote the general welfare—the general welfare of all Americans.

We are proud that this has been done without depriving one single American of one single liberty and without the socializing of any aspect of American life. We propose to continue to protect the rights of all individuals and to preserve our free enterprise economy. . . .

In the field of domestic legislative activity we shall continue the balanced program of conservation and integrated development

[3] From text of Democratic party's National Resolutions Committee statement approved at Chicago, May 16, 1950. New York *Times*. p19. May 17, 1950. Reprinted by permission.

of our natural resources which are the bedrock foundation of our economic society.

This means that we shall continue reclamation and flood control projects and that we shall continue to harness the energy of our streams to create the cheap electrical power that has been so important in encouraging economic expansion over many areas of our nation.

We believe that the pattern of integrated valley development pioneered by the Tennessee Valley—a project which has created wealth and productive capital far beyond its original cost—be continued in the valley of the Columbia River and in other areas where such a project is found feasible.

We recognize the croplands must be protected against the ravages of misuse or overuse by a program of soil conservation conducted vigorously and we also recognize that our farm economy must be kept healthy if the nation is to continue to progress.

We view as a serious problem the drop in the income and purchasing power of American farmers and reiterate that the Democratic party believes in supporting farm income at a fair level at a time when that support is needed and rejects the idea that supports should be high when they are not needed and low when they are needed.

We believe that our party should always be alert for methods to improve our farm program and we believe that a system of production payments on certain commodities as proposed by the President offers an excellent opportunity to improve our present program and should be given a test at the earliest possible opportunity.

We believe that competition is the life blood of our free enterprise economy and we stand for continued vigilance by the Department of Justice and other agencies charged with the job of preventing monopolistic practices and of encouraging competition.

We believe that changes improving the present antitrust laws can be of great value in preserving competition and assisting small business.

Further, in the field of small business, we call for a federal program which will enable private financial institutions to pro-

vide small business with the capital it needs to compete successfully with larger concerns.

We do not believe that big business in itself is bad for our
economy, but we believe that small business must be given the
opportunity to grow and thrive so that our economy can expand
as our population increases. We must preserve the kind of
America where a man with big and good ideas but small capital
can succeed in the world of business.

We believe that the working man must receive a fair return
for his labor if our economy is to remain in balance.

We hail the contributions minimum wage legislation has
made in this field and believe that existing laws should be under
constant study so that they may be changed as conditions warrant.

We believe that growth of the trade union movement has
contributed greatly to economic stability and to the expanded
economy and higher standards of living which all Americans now
enjoy.

The Taft-Hartley Law is unfair to labor unions and imperils
the contributions which organized labor has made to our society.
We urge its repeal and substitution therefor of legislation which
will be equally fair to worker and to management and will
protect the public interest by encouraging genuine collective bargaining.

Our employment insurance program should be strengthened
as a cushion against temporary recessions or local unemployment.

The program of federal assistance to the housing industry and
to public agencies desiring to construct low-cost housing for low-
income groups has contributed greatly both to the economic good
health of our nation and to the personal welfare of our citizens
by encouraging the family life in good surroundings that is a
tradition of our nation. This program must be continued and
additional steps should be taken to enable middle-income families
to achieve better homes at prices that will not work hardships
upon them.

Until the housing shortage which still exists in many areas is
alleviated, it is necessary to provide a reasonable system of rent
controls in order to prevent severe economic dislocation and
actual hardship on many families. The present law provides

for equitable adjustment of rents and for orderly decontrol and
should be continued until the present housing shortage is ended.

In other fields which contribute to the personal welfare of our
citizens the nation has made great strides but our successes in
these fields should not cause us to become complacent but rather
to spur us on toward even greater achievements.

Increased activity by the Federal Government is necessary in
the field of education to provide every American with the opportunity for a decent minimum of education.

Our Social Security system needs to be broadened and its
benefits increased.

In the field of health we need more hospitals, more doctors,
dentists and nurses, more medical technicians of every kind,
more research and more public health activities in connection
with medical care which will protect our citizens from the
financial disaster which illness can now bring to millions of
families.

In order to avoid socialized medicine in the United States, we
endorse the President's program for broadened federal activity in
the entire field of health and medical care and the adoption of
a pay-as-you-go insurance program to put better medical care
within the financial reach of all Americans.

"SURCEASE FROM APPREHENSIONS
AND ANXIETIES" [4]

If a free society is to win the battle for men's hearts and souls,
it must furnish surcease from the apprehensions and anxieties that
lead men to surrender their freedom for the phantom promises
of totalitarianism. The Fair Deal is doing this by furnishing
certain minimum basic securities. Our social security laws provide
minimum protection against the hazards of old age and unemployment. Through health insurance, we hope to provide protection from the catastrophe of sickness and disease, and
incidentally from the high cost of dying. Our housing laws will

---

[4] From address to *Herald Tribune* Annual Forum, by Federal Security Administrator Oscar R. Ewing, October 24, 1949. New York *Herald Tribune*. Sec. 10.
p12+. October 30, 1949.

give decent shelter to more and more of our people. Our minimum wage laws put a floor under wages so that men cannot be
forced to work for starvation pay. Federal aid to education, when
it comes, will help give every boy and girl equal educational
opportunities so that none will, except of their own accord,
remain the slaves of ignorance and the victims of industrial
incompetence.

These great programs of the Fair Deal will strengthen the
ring of freedom that centuries of struggle has drawn around
western man.

What is this freedom that the Fair Deal is designed to
strengthen? Fortunately, the tests of freedom have been phrased
in words of classic grandeur by Winston Churchill, who is
certainly no flaming radical. . . . I ask you to apply them to each
and every item of the Fair Deal program and you will see that
the program is completely within the framework of our cherished
freedoms.

Here are Churchill's words:

1. Is there the right to free expression of opinion and of
opposition and criticism of the government of the day?

2. Have the people the right to turn out a government of
which they disapprove, and are constitutional means provided by
which they can make their will apparent?

3. Are there courts of justice free from violence by the
executive and free from the threats of mob violence and all
association with any particular political parties?

4. Will these courts administer open and well-established
laws which are associated in the human mind with the broad
principles of decency and justice?

5. Will there be fair play for poor as well as for rich, for
private persons as well as government officials?

6. Will the rights of individuals, subject to their duties to
the state, be maintained and asserted and exalted?

7. Is the ordinary farmer or workman, earning a living by
daily toil and striving to bring up his family, free from the
fear that some grim police organization under control of a single
party, like the Gestapo, started by the Nazis and the Fascists, will

tap him on the shoulder and pack him off without fair or open trial to bondage or ill-treatment?

The Fair Deal answer to each one of Mr. Churchill's seven questions is yes—seven times yes. But these questions and their answers have another value. They enable you to judge the rubbish handed out by those who talk scornfully of statism and the welfare state as though the Fair Deal would destroy our freedom.

The fundamental purpose of the Fair Deal is to set men free, to free them from the haunting anxieties that destroy their peace of mind, to fulfill the promise of the Declaration of Independence that declares that man has certain inalienable rights, among which are life, liberty and the pursuit of happiness. Our opponents talk mostly of the right to liberty—generally their own liberty—and seem to forget that the right to life and the right to the pursuit of happiness are equally fundamental.[5] The right to life is something more than police protection from physical violence. The right to life means the right to a job, since few men can live without a livelihood. The right to life means the right to good health, since good health is fundamental to a full life. The right to life and the pursuit of happiness means a right to an education, since ignorance is the enemy of abundant living. The right to life means the right to security when the body is too old to work further, since life is hollow when it is surrounded by the anxieties of an end in the poorhouse.

The opponents of the Fair Deal fail to comprehend today's problems. They seem to have no understanding of any anxieties except their own. They interpret the slightest effort toward social change as the hot breath of revolution. They do not realize that a free society must offer positive answers to the haunting anxieties that beset modern man or else he is left vulnerable to the blandishments of totalitarianism.

Despite the opposition, the New Deal and the Fair Deal have met and will continue to meet these needs of our time. The New Deal took a land its opponents had left broken and despairing and gave it new confidence in itself. Those opponents

[5] Cf. "The Liberties We Are Losing," by Raymond Moley, in section on Dangers of the Welfare State.

had well-nigh destroyed man's faith in democracy as a workable way of life. The New Deal restored it. The Fair Deal would perfect it. Within the framework of every freedom that our ancestors and we have developed, the Fair Deal seeks to make the state a better servant of our people. Those of us who toil daily in the arena of practical politics know that perfection will never come, but we also know that, out of these daily struggles, slow and painful progress is being made and that the Fair Deal philosophy is leading us upward to a better America.

"BREAD AND FREEDOM CAN LIVE TOGETHER" [6]

We have learned at great cost in two world wars that people and freedom are indivisible. We have yet fully to learn that economic security and material well-being for the great mass of people are inseparably tied together with the struggle to make freedom, security and peace lasting in the world.

The selfish and socially irresponsible forces of reaction originally raised the question of the welfare state as a part of its scare campaign to block social progress in America. We can believe in the sovereignty of people over profits and must meet the challenge of reaction with a positive and practical program of social action which gives substance to the welfare state concept in terms of human and democratic values.

We are dedicated to the proposition that the highest duty of democratic government is to serve and advance the general welfare of the total community. Democratic government is the advancement of all the people. It must be made into an effective instrument which reflects our will and meets our needs. The forces of reaction on the extreme right and the extreme left would corrupt the high purpose of democratic government. The Communists would have us believe that economic security and the material well-being made possible by the welfare state cannot be achieved without sacrificing political and spiritual freedom. On the other hand, the socially irresponsible exponents of laissez-faire

[6] From an address by Walter P. Reuther, president, United Automobile Workers (CIO). Delivered before the League for Industrial Democracy, New York, April 15, 1950. Printed by permission.

economics would have us believe that human insecurity is the inevitable price that man must pay for freedom.

Those of us who believe in the welfare state must prove that both bread and freedom can live together in democracy's houses. American democracy will meet the challenge of the Cominform, not by an eloquent recitation of the pious virtues of democracy, but by a positive program of social action geared to the advancement of the welfare of the great mass of people. American democracy will be judged not by its noble promises but by its practical performance in terms of people and their welfare.

Those reactionary forces who today use the term welfare state with contempt have ever been willing and eager to accept government assistance to advance their own interests. When the RFC spent billions to bail out big business that was the highest achievement of Americanism, but when the same government is called upon to use its authority to procure and accept responsibility for the welfare of people—to provide federal aid to education, to provide decent housing, to take positive steps to meet the problem of growing unemployment, to provide minimum legislation and other necessary government action to meet the problems of the people, such action is labeled un-American and destructive to our democratic way of life. The argument in America is not whether the welfare state is to be or not to be. We have always had a welfare state. The argument fundamentally is whose welfare does the welfare state serve.

In the atomic age the state must necessarily be geared to the advancement of the welfare of the total people. This is not only a matter of economic and social justice. This is a matter of democratic survival. The cold war is a struggle for men's hearts and minds and their loyalties. The practical implementation of the broad humanitarian concept of the welfare state will provide us with our most potent weapon against totalitarianism both of the right and the left. In those parts of Europe where there is a strong, free democratic labor movement and where the state has accepted and carried out its broad social and moral responsibilities with respect to the welfare of the total people, the forces of democracy are strong and the forces of reaction and totalitarianism are weak. Where the state has been used as an instrument of special privilege, and the welfare of the great mass of people has been disregarded in those countries, democracy stands threatened by the growing power of reaction and totalitarianism.

Freedom and peace in the world will be made secure only to the extent that they rest on a broad foundation of economic and social justice. At the task of building that broad foundation the American economy is our strongest asset. Those blind forces of reaction in America who would lead us back down the road to so-called normalcy and commit the American economy to the economics of scarcity and special privilege are the Cominform's most valuable allies. These same blind forces, if permitted to grow unchecked in America, will drive us again to depression and disaster as they did in 1929, and provide the Cominform with a weapon more devastating than a stock pile of H-bombs. If we are to divert depression, war and disaster, we must prove that American democracy has the moral strength and the practical know-how to meet the threatening challenge of growing unemployment.

We who believe in democracy must demonstrate the faith, the will and determination to mobilize our human and material resources to achieve the abundance for the positive values of peace, freedom and human security as we mobilize our resources for the end of war and destruction. The H-bomb has created a serious moral and political vacuum in the world. We must fill that vacuum by a positive program of social action geared to the advancement of basic human and democratic values. Failure on our part will permit the apostles of fear and hate to create an atmosphere of uncertainty and hysteria which will make war inevitable.

The H-bomb did not create man's dilemma—it only served to dramatize it. Our dilemma is a reflection of the serious moral and cultural lag between man's progress in the physical sciences and his lack of comparable progress in the human and social sciences. We have learned to split the atom but we have as yet to learn to feed people when there is enough to eat in the world.

The broad humanitarian concept of the welfare state, translated into practical and tangible every day action will create the social mechanism through which we can establish a moral balance between man's achievement in the physical and in the social arena. Such a welfare state government would reflect the democratic will and provide the common agency that would assure the translation of technical progress into human progress, human security and human freedom and dignity.

"EXTINCTION OF SPECIAL PRIVILEGE" [7]

"Democracy," said one of the world's greatest men, "arose from men's thinking that if they are equal in any respect, they are equal absolutely." Those words were written more than two thousand years ago by a Greek named Aristotle. Those words define the welfare state as much as any phrase of Franklin D. Roosevelt or Harry S. Truman.

It has become fashionable in circles of political reaction to attack the concept of the welfare state as being prejudicial to individual liberty and freedom. These reactionaries view with fright and alarm the current and proposed activities of government in the fields of housing, health, and social security.

"These are steps on the road to communism," the alarmists cry. But ... I could cite laws and programs by the score enacted over the violent opposition of the reactionaries—laws and programs which were assailed as communistic at the time—but which are now accepted even in the most conservative circles.

This cry of state tyranny has been raised during the last half-century whenever the community has attempted to interfere with the right of a few to destroy forests, exploit little children, operate unsanitary and unsafe shops, indulge in race or religious discrimination, and pursue other policies endangering the health, safety and welfare of the community. These few have completely ignored the fact that, when their license to exploit the community was restricted, the freedom of the many from ignorance, insecurity, and want—the freedom of the many to live the good life—was measurably enhanced.

[7]From an address by Senator Herbert H. Lehman of New York. Delivered before the League for Industrial Democracy, New York, April 15, 1950. Printed by permission.

I do not believe that our Federal Government should seek to assume functions which properly belong to the individual or to the family, to the local community, or to free organizations of individuals. But I do believe that our Federal Government should and must perform those functions which, in this complex and interdependent society, the individual, the family, or the community cannot practicably perform for themselves.

Today we in America and in the entire freedom-loving world are confronted with a world-wide threat to that principle which we hold most dear, the principle of individual dignity and of individual freedom. For the preservation of that principle we are willing to dedicate our lives, if it should prove necessary. But while this is a threat which we face on the world front, we face another danger here at home. That is the threat to our freedom from those within our own country who would identify individual freedom with special privilege. Any move to diminish privilege, to stamp out discrimination and to bring security to our citizens is branded by these people as un-American.

Not so long ago an American political leader said that "the governments of the past could fairly be characterized as devices for maintaining in perpetuity the place and position of certain privileged classes. The government of the United States, on the other hand, is a device for maintaining in perpetuity the rights of the people, with the ultimate extinction of all privileged classes." Was it some Communist, some irresponsible radical or reformer who made that statement? No, it was not. It was the late President Calvin Coolidge in a speech at Philadelphia in 1924.

It is my firm belief that the extinction of special privilege is an essential and basic program of the welfare state. Today the forces of special privilege provide the chief opposition and raise the wildest cries of alarm against economic security for all.

In addition to the forces of special privilege who are opposed, on principle, to all social legislation, there are some who, while paying lip service to liberalism, claim to be troubled by the expanding scope of government in its direct concern with the welfare of the individual citizen. These people, while conceding merit to the specific programs of the welfare state, and while approving the welfare state programs of the past, join with the forces of privilege in contending that if the government provides any further services, it is moving in the direction of totalitarianism.

In my opinion these men of little vision have lost sight of the most important, and to me the most obvious, truth of our times— that a government which has secured the greatest degree of welfare for its people is the government which stands most firmly against totalitarianism. The critics of the welfare state do not understand this simple fact. They spend their time looking for Communists in and out of government and at the same time attack those measures which would deprive Communists and would-be Communists of their ammunition—and of their audience. The measures which would provide for the welfare of the people are the surest weapons against totalitarianism.

The Communist international, its leaders, and their philosophy, have been responsible for many designs which we in the democratic world consider the quintessence of evil. Certainly the suppression of basic rights—the police state and the slave labor camp—constitute the most repulsive and obnoxious way of life we can imagine.

But, as a liberal, I have a *special* resentment against the Communists. I feel that one of their greatest disservices to the cause of human progress has been their identification of economic security with the suppression of freedom. It is their claim that in order to achieve the solution of the economic needs of the many, it is necessary to curb the freedoms of all. They say, in effect, that you cannot have a full stomach and a free mind at the same time.

I reject this concept! I reject it as being the ultimate in reaction. This is but another demonstration of the basic affinity between Communists and reactionaries in their thinking about man and his problems. *Both* groups believe that a nation of free men cannot possibly conquer the scourges of hunger, disease, lack of shelter, intolerance and ignorance. And they *both* have much to gain if they convince enough people that freedom and security are incompatible.

It is a strange paradox that the same conservatives and re-actionaries who pose as champions of national security express the greatest antagonism toward individual security. Most of us readily acknowledge that the nations of the world cannot be free if they are not secure. It seems equally logical to me that *individuals* cannot be free if they are beset by fear and insecurity. To my mind the welfare state is simply a state in which people are free to develop their individual capacities, to receive just awards for their talents, and to engage in the pursuit of hap-piness, unburdened by fear of actual hunger, actual homelessness or oppression by reason of race, creed, or color.

The fear of old age, the fear of sickness, the fear of un-employment, and the fear of homelessness are not—as some would have us believe—essential drives in a productive society. These fears are not necessary to make free competitive enterprise work. The fear of insecurity is rather a cancer upon free com-petitive enterprise. It is the greatest threat which confronts our economic system. I hasten to add that I believe in free com-petitive enterprise. I believe it is the best system yet devised by man. But it is not a goal in itself. It must always serve the public interest.

We have had [nearly] twenty years of the New Deal and the Fair Deal. Who would say that the American worker, the American farmer and the ordinary American businessman is less free than he was twenty years ago? Actually, freedom in the true sense flourishes more generally and more widely today than ever before in our history. The worker, the farmer and the businessman have vastly more freedom than they ever had before. They are freer to enjoy the fruits and benefits of a productive economy and a full life. But they are not yet free enough.

We are still far from the goal we seek. Insecurity still haunts millions. Inadequate housing poisons the wells of family life in vast numbers of cases. Inadequate schooling handicaps a great segment of our people. And the fear of sickness and old age still clutches at the hearts of many if not most of our fellow citizens. Until we solve all these probems and quiet all these fears, our people will not be truly free.

"A SOUND CONSTITUTIONAL PATH" [8]

Collectivism is the public ownership of the means of production and distribution. Under it, the state would own and operate the railroads, mines, manufacturing establishments, banks, and insurance companies. Under the most sweeping definition of collectivism, the state would also own and operate farms, retail stores and wholesale establishments; and virtually all members of the professions, such as doctors, dentists, teachers and journalists, would also be employed by the state. . . .

It is obvious that, far from traveling a dangerous road to "collectivism," the United States is continuing to follow a sound constitutional path. Our industries are privately owned and operated, with the exception of the roads, the schools and a small portion of electrical power. No responsible person proposes that this be altered. We all want to make the system of so-called free enterprise work.

But there are certain pubic functions directly confided to the national government by the Constitution. The preamble to that document states very explicitly that in addition to forming a "more perfect Union," there were four specific ends which the new government was to further. These were: to "establish justice, insure domestic tranquility, provide for the common defense, promote the general welfare." . . .

The duty of providing for all of these purposes (including the general welfare) was thus made part of the basic obligation of the government. It is our task to see what those basic purposes require today and how these requirements are being fulfilled.

The establishment of justice involves more than the mere creation of courts and the machinery of civil and criminal justice. It is something that must be established in our material affairs—in the market place, the bank and the factory; on the railroads and over the air waves. And justice must be sought as much in advance of grievances as after the occurrence of wrong.

[8] From "Are We Headed Toward 'Collectivism'?" by Senators Harry F. Byrd of Virginia and Paul H. Douglas of Illinois. New York *Times Magazine.* p7+. December 18, 1949. This selection is from Senator Douglas' reply to two questions posed by the *Times*, (1) "What is your own definition of collectivism?" and (2) "Do you believe we are headed toward what you call collectivism?"— Editor.

Thus we have an Interstate Commerce Commission, which seeks to protect shippers and common carriers; a Federal Trade Commission, which stands guard against unfair trade practices and seeks to stimulate competition in order that we may have a free society. The Food and Drug Administration tries to protect consumers from injurious or spurious products. The Federal Communications Commission protects public rights in and over the air waves. The Securities and Exchange Commission seeks to safeguard the investor and the National Labor Relations Board substitutes the principle of collective bargaining for that of all-out industrial warfare. Further means by which justice is established in this country could be adduced almost endlessly.

The insurance of domestic tranquility no longer means the use of federal troops to put down a bloody strike. We, in this country, have learned from the events of the depression the relationship existing between internal order and the degree to which individuals may satisfy their basic wants. It was to insure our domestic tranquility that a series of stabilizing actions were undertaken by the Roosevelt and Truman administrations—and these in the face of bitter Republican and conservative opposition.

I need only recall the unemployment insurance programs, designed to take the terror out of joblessness and help maintain purchasing power during recession or depression; the guarantee of bank deposits to protect individual savings, at the same time permitting banks to follow more liberal credit policies in periods of stress. There are the Federal Housing Administration guarantees in the field of private housing which have provided the strongest stimulus in our history to the building of homes and have been greatly beneficial, both economically and spiritually. Again, the protection given farm prices has prevented a downward plummeting at crucial points, has given the farmer an incentive to produce and has prevented a breakdown of farm purchasing power.

All but the most extreme of pacifists would agree that provision for the common defense is a primary function of government. But few seem to realize that these costs [prior to an additional $15 billion commitment for Korea and elsewhere in summer of 1950] run to approximately $34 billion in the current fiscal year, or more than three quarters of our budget.

This sum is composed of $15 billion for the armed services, $1.5 billion for rearming the European democracies, about $1 billion for atomic energy, $5.5 billion for economic aid to the nations resisting communism and for the costs of occupying Germany and Japan. Then we should add to this the interest on the war-incurred public debt, which comes to about $5 billion, and veterans' benefits and costs, which amount to $6 billion more. Only about $10 billion will be spent on all other purposes of government.

We live in a "warfare world," so to speak, rather than in a "welfare state.". . . I deplore such huge expenditures, but they were created neither by President Roosevelt nor President Truman. To the degree that personal guilt is involved we should charge them up to Kaiser Wilhelm, Adolf Hitler, Karl Marx and Joseph Stalin.

In listening to attacks upon the so-called "welfare state," I have been struck by the derisive manner in which these words are employed. The way these words are commonly hissed out shows an ignorance of the Constitution, which told our lawmakers to provide for the general welfare. No such derisive overtones were heard when the Federal Government made lavish grants of land to build railroads or to encourage the marvelous growth of state universities. Nor could they be detected when the Federal Government took the lead in the construction of roads, in soil conservation and protection from forest fires; in flood control, the dredging of rivers and harbors and the building of levees; or the furnishing of vital information to business and agriculture.

Why, then, after a hundred and fifty years, should an honorable word like "welfare" suddenly become a synonym for the devil? The answer is a simple one. As long as it was the welfare of the propertied classes that was being advanced, the word stood as Holy Writ. But the horrors of the "welfare state" were shouted from the roof-tops when the Federal Government began to spend money to aid the great groups in our society that had little or no property. The total cost of welfare items in the coming year amounts to only $2.2 billion—about 5 per cent of the total federal budget and about 1 per cent of the net national income.

TURNABOUT ON "SOMETHING FOR NOTHING" [9]

The phrase "something for nothing" was used thirty years ago in denunciation of big business; it was applied to the grabbing and scheming of financial barons to evade the rules of fair competition.

By a curious semantic somersault "something for nothing" has been taken up today and put to use as a missile by the spokesmen of big business and political conservatism to hurl at what they call the "gimme" attitude of the common folks toward government. A popular phrase among liberals of the Progressive era of Theodore Roosevelt and Woodrow Wilson in their criticism of "the interests," it now bristles in condemnation of the "welfare state," the federal health insurance proposal, and the pension issue in labor disputes. The words themselves, however, remain the same.

Recent issues of *Time* and the New York *Herald Tribune* illustrate this reversal. *Time,* for example, quoted an unidentified midwest industrial executive who was exercised about union pension demands: "Our whole system is degenerating to the point where something for nothing is a fad. . . . The mad scramble is to be one of the fortunate few . . . on the receiving end. . . . Union leaders are playing the role of a master of ceremonies on a give-away program."

The *Herald Tribune,* more sanguine than *Time's* businessman, commented favorably on a statement regarding pensions issued by Irving S. Olds, chairman of the board of directors of the U. S. Steel Company: "What Mr. Olds called the 'Santa Claus' idea of pensions is one which in the long run is not likely to appeal to labor any more than to the natural instincts of the American people. . . . The desire to get something for nothing is not characteristic of the American people."

The conservatives, it seems, are now busy at the old game of stealing their opponents' clothes while the latter are bathing. It is the liberals, beyond a doubt, who have traditionally used "something for nothing" as their battle cry in the struggles

[9] An article by Robert H. Bremner, instructor in history, Ohio State University. *Survey.* 86:73-5. February 1950. Reprinted by permission.

against privileged interests. Could it be that this new usage of "something for nothing" is part of a campaign to disguise reaction in the trappings of liberalism? At any rate a comparison of the meaning of the phrase during the Progressive era with its usage today will prove enlightening.

The elder Robert M. LaFollette, of Wisconsin, was referring to business, not labor, when he said in 1913 that friendly legislation of all kinds made it "easier to grow rich by gifts from the government than by efficient service and honest effort." President Wilson, in his tariff message the same year warned of the possibility of "a complete loss of the influences that quicken enterprise and keep independent energy alive." Wilson was thinking, not of the debilitating effects of aid to the farmer, or of pension plans for workers, or of socialized medicine, but of the "set of privileges and exemptions from competition" behind which he thought monopoly flourished. As a result of the freedom from competition which had been obtained by such measures as the protective tariff, Wilson believed that the point had been reached where "nothing is normal, nothing is obliged to stand the tests of efficiency and economy in our world of big business, but everything thrives by concerted arrangement."

Frederic C. Howe, later U. S. Commissioner of Immigration, a political scientist and lawyer and an expert in municipal government, used privilege and monopoly as synonymous terms. In an interesting little volume entitled *The Confessions of a Monopolist*, published in 1906, Howe cited public utility franchises, tariff advantages, railway control, and tax evasions as examples of monopoly. Only by means of such special favors, he maintained, can wealth be obtained without labor. Not the copybook maxims of thrift and industry, but "make society work for you," "make the other fellow pay," "get something for nothing"— these, Howe asserted, are the guiding principles of the monopolist.

Howe, like many of the Progressives, was indebted to the single tax theories of Henry George for his introduction to the idea of something for nothing. George's concept of the unearned increment of land values provided a classic example of the method by which individuals can pocket socially created wealth. In his treatment of the ethics of private ownership in land, George repeatedly emphasized the injustice of permitting land-holders to profit from the exertions of those who used their land. He denounced rent as the device which "strips the many of the wealth they justly earn, to pile it up in the hands of the few, who do nothing to earn it."

Thorstein Veblen, whose influence on New Dealers may be compared to that of Henry George on the Progressives, made frequent use of "something for nothing." In *The Vested Interests and the State of the Industrial Arts*, Veblen defined a vested interest as "a marketable right to get something for nothing." Veblen also used the term "free income" to describe money derived from intangible assets such as good will, monopoly rights, or outstanding corporation securities He referred to the possessors of vested interests or of free income as "the kept classes" "who derive an income from the established order of ownership and privilege."

Among the arguments most frequently directed against the welfare state is the contention that once common action has banished the specter of insecurity, individuals will lose the quality of initiative which has been nurtured under the system of self-help. Robert Hunter, the author of *Poverty* (published in 1912), devoted much attention to the physical and moral degeneration of that portion of the population which lived habitually and entirely upon charity. He described the flabby, "pot-bellied and pigeon-breasted" vagrants he had observed under the showers at municipal lodging houses. He added:

> One can readily see the meaning of these physical characteristics. They are the result of lack of work and purpose. They are the effect of sensualism and debauch. The tramp, instead of developing himself by struggle to overcome the obstacles of poverty, has evaded responsibilities and duties, and has traveled the line of least resistance.

Hunter likened pauperism to parasitism and called it a "disease of character." But he insisted also that pauperism, that is, the practice of existing off the largess of society, was not confined to the poor. He wrote:

While poverty unquestionably is the soil, as it were, in which pauperism may most readily grow, pauperism itself is not peculiar to the poor; it is also a disease of the rich. Mr. C. S. Loch, the ablest student of this subject in England, considers that pauperism is a moral and not an economic question, and the first it unquestionably is. An important book written by two professors of the University of Brussels on *Parasitism, Organic and Social* gives instances of widespread pauperism or parasitism existing in all classes of society. The people of tropical countries have often been called the "Paupers of Nature" because life has been made easy for them, and means of livelihood have been supplied them at certain times and places without any effort on their part. The idle rich have also been called paupers. . . .

The parasitism of the capitalist class was a favorite theme of many popular writers during the Progressive era. David Graham Phillips, the novelist and muckraker, ascribed the critical ferment of his day to the resentment of the middle class toward a social system under which "the masses have to work for what they get, while a small class gets more than enough without work." The poet, Edwin Markham, protested that "the people support a horde of rich idlers and wasters, who get and get but give nothing." Markham announced that he looked forward to the day when "we shall not use men to make money but shall use money to make men." Alfred Henry Lewis, a staunch but cynical individualist, decried "this tipping system, this trying to get something for which you have not worked." In his opinion, Chauncey M. Depew and other servants of corporate interests in Congress were merely "big tip takers."

Frederick Townsend Martin, himself a member of the leisure class, was disturbed by the widening chasm between capital and labor. In *The Passing of the Idle Rich* he criticized the tendency of some of his friends to scoff at the agitation of the working class for a more equitable distribution of wealth. It is erroneous, he warned, to compare the demand of the American worker for a job and decent wages to the cry of the Roman mob for bread and coin. In Rome, the pauperized mass was a race of parasites who could be fed or crushed as the occasion demanded. In America, on the other hand, the masses are the producing elements of the country while the rich, who live off the proceeds of corporate holdings are the parasites.

One of the more ironic aspects of the present adoption of "something for nothing" by the conservatives is that the phrase once served as the theme of a book by John Peter Altgeld. Reviled by the conservatives of his own time, it is most unlikely that Altgeld's social views and sympathies would recommend him any more highly to the conservatives of today. His book, *The Cost of Something for Nothing*, attempted to apply the laws of biology and physics to human conduct. Altgeld maintained that getting something for nothing not only bred "the germs of dissolution" but also violated "the eternal law of equivalents, the universal law of balance."

Altgeld recognized two types of parasites among human beings: One is the flunky who behaves in a servile fashion in order to secure favors from his master; the other is "the insidious parasite whom conditions or institutions have placed in a position where he can suck the substance of other people's toil." Altgeld was particularly interested in the effect of parasitism on the parasite: "The man who eats bread that is earned by others is a parasite; in the social economy he is but a sack with a sucking mouth. Not being compelled to exert his other organs or faculties, they cease to grow."

Louis D. Brandeis, Hunter, Wilson, and LaFollette also expressed concern over the loss of efficiency occasioned by parasitism in the business world. In general however, the Progressives were less interested in the individual than in the social effects of something for nothing. Tom L. Johnson, the single-tax mayor of Cleveland, put the blame for most vice and crime on the condition he called "involuntary poverty." He believed that involuntary poverty resulted from "law-made privilege whereby some get more than they earn while the mass of mankind earns more than it makes." Frederic C. Howe, who was one of Johnson's lieutenants in the fight against privilege in Cleveland, voiced the same objection to monopoly: by stifling competition, monopoly curtails opportunity and thereby produces unemployment. Similarly, the blunt implication behind Veblen's fine-spun prose was that in our present society we suffer periodic depression and unemployment because our economic activity is not designed to meet the needs of the community but rather to produce "free income" for the "kept" classes.

Taking something for nothing has not seemed always and everywhere so reprehensible as it does to Americans. Indeed, during many epochs of history it has appeared prefectly natural, just, and proper that certain classes or castes, by reason of birth or profession, should enjoy advantages denied to the common man. In the United States, however, belief in the fundamental equality of men, in the dignity of labor, and in the necessity of work to the full development of personality has led us to condemn the search for the special favors which confer a privileged status. As the historian, James Truslow Adams, has pointed out, Americans have always lusted after property but have hated privilege. According to Adams' definition, privilege means "the obtaining of property not by brains, hard work, or in any other legitimate way, but just by 'drag.' "

How valid is the current use of "something for nothing"? There is no possible denial that looking to the government for economic assistance is more widespread today than ever before. Even the most cursory study of American politics in the past two decades proclaims its vast increase.

Labor and agriculture have joined the businessman in seeking the advantages of friendly legislation. There has been such a surge of "wanting" among the masses of men that, according to some, we are all privilege-seekers now. This is disconcerting indeed to groups which in the past were the exclusive recipients of legal privilege.

The clear meaning, it seems to me, is that larger and larger sections of the public have come to appreciate useful functions to which a democratic government can be put. The ruling classes always have looked upon government with a pragmatic eye and judged its value by the services it rendered them. When the ruling class is small, the favors it enjoys may rightly be considered as privileges. But when the ruling group is widely distributed and when the services furnished by the government are made available to all, privilege is not an accurate accusation. *The essence of privilege is limited, or restricted, or exclusive enjoyment of a favor.* On the other hand, a vigorous widespread demand for the use of politics as a means of advancing the welfare of all the people is actually a guarantee that government will not be subverted to private, class, or party benefit.

MONOPOLY—NOT WELFARE—THREATENS AMERICA [10]

We are moving into the second half of the twentieth century, a century which has seen America's productive strength grow beyond the dreams of even the most visionary of our national founders. Today we have the natural resources and the technical knowledge to open up a new vista. President Truman's recent messages to Congress have demonstrated the possibilities that are open to us. Merely by continuing our past rate of growth we can within five years increase in production 20 per cent, which would mean increasing the average family income by about $1,000 a year. Within our grasp in the next fifty years we can treble today's standard of living which would mean average family incomes of $12,000 a year.

We have an opportunity for the first time in the world's history to establish a society in which every family can have a decent standard of living and in which luxury living will be available to an increasing number of our citizens. It can be a society in which all have enough without unduly limiting the rewards available for the more industrious and the more able.

Yet as these possibilities come to mind, there also comes to mind the increasing complexity of our society.

In the not too distant past opportunity was open to all. If a man was willing to make the effort he could have the richest land and the richest resources for the asking.

Today millions of families are dependent on jobs that may disappear tomorrow with no others available. Millions of families live on tiny worn-out farms eking out a bare subsistence.

[10] From an address by Senator Hubert H. Humphrey of Minnesota. Delivered before the Harvard Law School Forum, Cambridge, Mass., March 24, 1950. Printed by permission.

In this the land of plenty—in this the century of progress —we in America still have almost ten million families, or about one quarter of our population, trying to get along on less than $2,000 a year.

Here is the crisis we face. Here is why we need a Fair Deal program working toward an increasing welfare program, working toward greater economic democracy.

There are some who feel that the realization of the dream which is before our eyes cannot be achieved without sacrificing the free enterprise system—and they prefer the free enterprise system.

They are of little faith. I believe in the free enterprise system —I am not a Socialist. No other system could have made the progress we have made in the past hundred and fifty years. But the free enterprise system in America as we have seen it has always been one receiving encouragement, stimulation, and protection from government activity—from government welfare programs.

Let us not forget that the protective tariff, the darling of big business for so many years, was one of the most flagrant examples of government interference in behalf of business.

The greatest threat to the free enterprise system in America is not social security, minimum wage, aid to education, rural electrical programs, and the like. The greatest threat to free enterprise in America is growing monopoly in America.

There are those who would have us believe that an unbalanced budget spells the end of free enterprise in America. That is nonsense. I am more concerned about the fact that the Federal Trade Commission recently reported to Congress another half a dozen industries which are dominated by four to six companies making a total of nineteen highly concentrated industries out of twenty-six studied. I am more concerned that three companies control 95.3 per cent of the tin can and other tinware industry; that three companies control 92.1 per cent of the linoleum industry; that another three companies control 88.5 per cent of the copper smelting and refining industry. In this connection Anaconda Copper alone controls almost half the capital assets of the whole industry and another quarter of the capital assets of the copper industry is controlled by Kennecott Copper Corporation.

I am concerned about the future of the free enterprise system when I learn from the Federal Trade Commission reports that a hundred and thirteen companies, all with assets of more than $100 million, own almost half of the manufacturing plant and equipment in the whole of our United States.

The free enterprise system is in danger but the danger does not arise from welfare programs. The danger arises from the fact that from 1940 through 1948, according to the Federal Trade Commission, more than 2,450 formerly independent firms in the manufacturing and mining industries alone disappeared as a result of merger and acquisitions. The asset value of these firms amounted to about $5.2 billion or nearly 5 per cent of the total asset value of our manufacturing corporations in America. Moreover, nearly one third of the companies merged were absorbed by the very largest corporations, those with assets exceeding $50 million.

It is monopoly which threatens a free America. I do not consider unbalanced budgets to be desirable objectives. Unbalanced national budgets however are no indication of the basic health of the American economy. The Republicans would balance the budget but they would do so, I suggest, at the expense of unbalancing the American economy. I remember well the days of the balanced budget under Ogden Mills, Andrew Mellon, and Herbert Hoover, and I remember that those balanced budgets spelled unbalanced family life for millions of Americans. I am more concerned with balancing the daily lives of Americans and their families so that they have full employment; so that they can enjoy the fruits of their labor; so that they can participate in the good life which is possible in our society.

If the Republican party should succeed in its program of opposition to social welfare legislation, if it should succeed in its efforts to curtail government expenditures at the expense of the middle and low income families of America, if it continues to advocate a "favor the rich" tax program such as the one it enacted when it was in power during the 80th Congress and which incidentally was primarily responsible for the unbalanced budget of the last two years—the Republican party will be the threat to free enterprise in America.

I recall the prophetic vision of Theodore Roosevelt when he said, "If socialism ever comes to America the Republican party will bring it."

I realize this sounds like a facetious statement to many but to me the only real safeguard for America, its freedoms and its economy, is a welfare program for America—a state which is concerned with *real* protection of free enterprise to the point of controlling monopoly, and a state which protects the American citizen from being governed by private corporations. We must have a government which wants to raise the standard of living for everyone, not just increase the wealth of the industrialists and financiers. We must have recognition of a man's right to work at a living wage. . . .

The philosophy of the welfare state . . . aims to satisfy at least four major objectives:

1. A comprehensive social insurance program including insurance and provision against the hazards of old age, disability, unemployment and costs of medical care.

2. Prevention or mitigation of unemployment through public works planning and monetary and fiscal policies.

3. Improvement of the standard of living through such programs as slum clearance and public housing and by providing better facilities and opportunities for education.

4. Limitations on the growth of powerful corporate enterprise with a view to protecting the interests of small business firms and less privileged elements within our society.

This issue of welfare state brings a vision to my mind. This vision symbolizes the choice which the American people face. On the one hand are those who would judge America and its accomplishments in terms of balance sheets and accounting records. On the other hand are those who judge America by its concrete accomplishments and by the happiness of its people. Those who oppose the welfare state remind me of the frightened men totting up their balances while the American people continue to go forward, build dams, and houses and electric and telephone lines.

In conclusion . . . I make a plea for a rational rather than an emotional approach to the problems of government. I make a plea that we respect the facts.

It is difficult for the American people to understand when Mr. Alfred P. Sloan, Jr., head of the Board of General Motors, makes a statement on January 15, 1950: "In recent years economic incentive has been weakened by the ever increasing take of government. I fear the effect is beginning to be felt on the economy." And then for General Motors to announce that it had earned $600 million profits in 1949—more than any other company has ever made in the history of American industry. I suggest this is not a rational approach to discussing political issues.

Since the war American big business, according to the Federal Trade Commission has been making approximately 20 per cent profit on its invested capital after taxes. This compares with about half that figure before the war.

If our political opponents wish to label the program we stand for as a welfare state—then let it be so. Call it what you will— one fact, however, stands out in bold relief. This program has raised the living standards of American people. It has given a modicum of security to all areas of our population. It has provided a floor on living standards. It is furnishing relief from the apprehensions and anxieties which lead men to surrender their freedom. It is providing minimum protection against the hazard of old age and unemployment. It will provide prevention from catastrophe of sickness and disease. It is giving decent shelter to more and more of our people. It is putting a floor under wages. It *will* provide federal aid to education so as to give every boy and girl equal educational opportunities so that none will remain the slaves of ignorance.

These programs are strengthening the ring of freedom that centuries of struggle has drawn around western man.

These programs are providing the incentive and will set the example which will undermine totalitarianism wherever it may be.

UNDERWRITING CERTAIN LEVELS [11]

Since the welfare state seems to be coming to occupy a dominant role in our domestic political discussions, it may be well for us to try to figure out what it really means. . . .

Certainly if, as the conservatives say, the welfare state is just a system of government handouts to any groups politically powerful enough to insist upon them, then even the most extreme liberal would be foolish to deny that such a system could harm. Handouts could easily create a dependence on the state that might sap the individual initiatives upon which free society depends, and, if the handouts were calculated, not according to economic plan, but according to political blackmail, they might well result in a grave weakening of the financial structure. The old age pension schemes in California, Oregon, and Washington, for example, seem to be an example of a handout system running amuck.

Yet, if such a system of government handouts does represent . . . our greatest internal danger, it may be permissible to ask how that system got started. History provides an unambiguous answer. It started when Alexander Hamilton wrote his famous reports on public finance, the national bank, and manufactures in the early years of the republic. Hamilton argued that the nation could not survive and prosper unless special government favors gave the business community a large stake in that survival and prosperity. Until Andrew Jackson destroyed the early nineteenth century federal improvements system with the Maysville veto—which forbade the use of national funds for a Kentucky highway—the Hamiltonian handout theory remained substantially dominant in Washington. And the Maysville veto did not affect handouts by the states where local governments provided lavish aid and facilities to private business through the first half of the nineteenth century. . . .

The handout system once started by Hamilton was irrevocably imbedded in government tradition by the Republican party after

[11] From "The Welfare State," by Arthur M. Schlesinger, Jr., associate professor of history, Harvard University. *Reporter*. 1:28-30. October 11, 1949. Reprinted by permission.

the Civil War. The most spectacular form of handout was the protective tariff, which preserved favored business undertakings from the hazards of free enterprise and gave them a huge annual subsidy levied on the American people. The grant of public lands to private railroad companies was a form of handout only slightly less appalling. The great conservative publicist of that day, Edwin L. Godkin, protested eloquently against the handout system. He warned the businessmen who were feeding so hungrily at the public trough that they ought not to complain if the farmers and workers eventually got the idea and followed their hoggish example. But men like Godkin were ignored; the system developed, and reached one of its climaxes in 1930 with the Smoot-Hawley tariff. That tariff was converted into law by the willing signature of President Herbert Hoover.

This history raises the interesting question of why Hoover and the other enemies of the welfare state should find favors so reprehensible when bestowed by government upon farmers or workers, and so beneficial when bestowed upon business. The answer, of course, is that the Hoover case against a system of government handouts is based on the comfortable theory that government aid to business is wise and virtuous, while government aid to the nonbusiness groups is vicious and leads to collectivism. . . .

The only consistent position against the handout system was that held by Godkin—that government should do nothing for any special group. This position has had no reality in American experience and has certainly never been advocated by the American business community.

Thus far most people have considered the welfare state on the evaluation of its opponents. I wonder whether that evaluation is very accurate, either in theory or in practice. The welfare state has a distinct and definable character. Briefly, it is a system wherein government agrees to underwrite certain levels of employment, income, education, medical aid, social security, and housing for all its citizens. The government does not try to do all these things itself; it seeks where possible to supplement the initiatives of private society. But it does accept the ultimate re-

sponsibility of guaranteeing "floors" in certain crucial areas, below which it conceives tolerable living to be impossible. And
it will intervene when private society demonstrates its incapacity
to maintain these minimum standards.

This is all that is meant by a welfare state. It should be
added perhaps, that western society came to the welfare state,
not through an excess of starry-eyed do-goodism nor, on the
other hand, through a sinister desire to lull an unsuspecting
people into totalitarianism. Western society was driven to welfarism by the most powerful and stark of all motives: fear. It
became evident early in our century that any government that
rejected responsibility for the welfare of all its citizens would
forfeit the loyalty of those whom it neglected. It was the overwhelming need to bribe the masses into remaining loyal—not
sentimental idealism—that created the welfare state. In the last
analysis, welfarism is a form of social Machiavellianism designed
to prevent the population from being harried, by insecurity,
poverty, and despair, into the arms of Fascists or Communists.
"If you do not give the people social reform," as an English
Tory has said, "the people will give you social revolution."

Who is really opposed to the welfare state today? I cannot
believe that it has many serious opponents left. "England and
the United States," one senator recently remarked, "have always
recognized the interest of the state in providing a decent minimum standard of living in food, clothing, medical care, and education for those unfortunate enough not to be able to pay for it
in full themselves. Housing is only an extension of the same
principle to decent shelter, which certainly is absolutely necessary
if the children are to have anything like equality of opportunity."
The speaker was Senator Robert A. Taft, a clear if sometimes
grudging champion of the essential principles of welfarism.

"We are all Hussites without knowing it," Martin Luther
cried centuries ago, suddenly discovering how far he had drifted
from Roman orthodoxy. So today we are all supporters of the
welfare state, as laissez-faireism has receded into the mythical
past. . . .

This agreement on the principle of ultimate government responsibility does not, of course, mean that there are no differences on domestic policy between Senator Taft and President Truman. Their differences are large and bitter; but they are not over the welfare state. The two main points of debate are over the type of government intervention and over the level at which the minimum standards are to be pegged. Senator Taft wants the states rather than the Federal Government to play the greater role in maintaining the "floors" under society.

Thus Taft accepts the principle of the minimum-wage law, but he boggled at the enlarged coverage which the Administration tried to write into the recent bill. He accepts the principle of government support for medical care; but he wants the care to be dispensed as much as possible through the states and to be confined to the needy rather than to be available to all. He may seek to eviscerate the fundamental conception, but he does not reject it. . . .

For better or for worse, the welfare state is with us. The great issue is whether it will become a matter of bread and circuses; and this possibility imposes a responsibility upon serious politicians of both the right and the left. This responsibility is not discharged by demagogic assaults upon the welfare state, any more than it is discharged by promiscuous demands for more pensions, more tariffs, more handouts. It can be discharged only when people settle down in an earnest attempt to meet the requirements of welfarism within a society that can remain free and prosperous. And this can be done only when each of the important special groups—and this means the business community fully as much as it means the farm bloc and the trade unions—recognizes that it cannot blindly pursue its own narrow interest without threatening irreparable harm to society as a whole.

DANGERS OF THE WELFARE STATE

WELFARE STATE ON THE RISE [1]

How . . . is this American version of socialism—the welfare state—being brought about?

Here are ten ways:

1. The income tax: Under the progressive income tax, incomes after taxes are undergoing a powerful leveling process. During the New Deal there was much talk of putting an upper limit of $25 thousand on individual incomes. The idea is not dead. The figure may be lowered.

Under the "ability to pay" theory of taxation, so long as Smith has more income left after taxes than Jones, Smith has still further ability to pay more taxes. There is no logical stopping place. The logical end of this tax philosophy is the final equalization of all incomes. This final position may be avoided, however, because the tax policymakers themselves are likely to continue to have above-average incomes and might not deem it "morally" or "economically" wise to go thus far.

But even this check can be made ineffectual by the simple device of having the politicians vote themselves ever bigger tax-free "expense" accounts! Then they can live well off these growing taxless expense accounts. Unlike the rest of us, they won't feel the full impact of a steadily rising income tax. A natural check on the leveling of income will disappear. Many salaries in the United Nations and in its various subsidiary organizations are made tax free. We have just given the President another $50,000 annual income free from all taxes (besides an increase in salary). Perhaps we have just seen the beginning of this wrinkle in the income-socializers' bag of tricks.

[1] From "Our Rising Welfare State," by Dr. Emerson P. Schmidt, director, Economic Research Department, Chamber of Commerce of the United States. *Nation's Business.* 37:29-31. April 1949.

The corporation income tax likewise takes a larger toll from the bigger corporate income than from the smaller. . . . There is constant pressure for an "excess" profits tax to "soak the rich" although the poorer citizen is just as likely to own a few shares in a profitable corporation as in one that is less profitable!

2. Social security: Employees, generally, pay 1 per cent [2] of the payroll to finance social security while employers pay 3 to 6 per cent or more, depending on how you figure it—covering workmen's compensation, old age and unemployment compensation. To some extent, social security is a device for spreading income more evenly over a period of time—collecting the premiums during employment and paying out benefits when hazard hits. But, the benefit formulas are generally loaded in favor of the low-income groups. Nearly all social security programs also have the effect of transferring income from the more productive, more efficient or more fortunate people to those less favorably disposed. The proposed expansion of social security suggests that this method of leveling income may be still in its infancy. We have covered only part of the distance between the cradle and the grave.

3. Federal variable grants-in-aid: In the hospital construction law, the amount of federal grants to the different states is based in part on average per capita incomes within the state, the bigger slice going to those states where incomes are lowest. The people in the "rich" states thus pay the hospital construction costs of the people in the "poor" states. In earlier years Federal grants for the aged, the blind, and dependent children were based on some uniform or equal-matching principle. Today it is rare for a Federal grant-in-aid bill to be introduced in Congress without a so-called variable grant-in-aid, the amount of the grant varying inversely with the per capita income among the different states. . . .

4. Food allotment: During the depression, with a view both to relief and to transferring more income to farm groups, the "orange and blue" food stamp allotment program was adopted. The extra stamps were the equivalent of good cash to those who

---

[2] Changed to 1.5 per cent on January 1, 1950.—Editor

got them. A bill recently introduced in Congress would revive this program. Clearly, this opens far-reaching avenues for the further redistribution of income and greater equalization. The law, or more likely the administrative bureau, could decide that all persons with less than so much annual income would get so many stamps entitling them to so much free goods.

5. Rent control: Rent control is a device for transferring income from people who supply housing to people who don't. New York State did not abolish the rent control growing out of World War I until 1927. The hold which rent control has on the American people today suggests that this method of redistributing income is likely to be difficult to remove even though all the evidence shows that it accentuates the desire for housing and diminishes the supply of new construction, especially in the face of the threat of extending rent controls to new construction.

6. Public housing: Again and again it is argued that private effort cannot provide adequate housing for the lowest income group. The government must come to the rescue, and the government must tax the people with more income so that the low-income groups can live in new housing.

7. Driving down the interest rate: Thrift and savings formerly were rewarded by annual interest earnings of about 5 per cent. Insurance premiums earned the same interest accumulations.

Today, interest rates have been cut in half by means of what is called monetary and fiscal policy, a subject a little complicated and subtle, but something we should study a little more.

In the past, periods of prosperity and especially war periods always entailed rising interest rates to help check excessive demand for borrowings and to stimulate the supply of savings. World War II was financed with a constant and low or falling interest rate. This was indeed a stupendous and far-reaching achievement.

Lord Keynes was the father of the engineered, artificially low interest rate which reduces the earning power of capital and savings. This transfers a greater portion of the earnings of capital to low-income groups.

Keynes spoke frequently of the "euthanasia of the *rentier*" and the "functionless investor." This was an erudite way of saying that there is really no point in paying anybody to save—adequate capital should and could be made available without anyone seemingly having to pay for it.

While he had some misgivings about his own brilliance on this point, his followers adhere rigidly to policies designed to make borrowing cheaper even though the policy reflects itself in a steady dilution of the money supply and a steady deterioration in the value of the dollar. Perhaps Keynes, and especially his followers, did not notice that driving down the interest rate also creates a new problem (or should we say, opportunity?) for the government, in the form of more old-age dependence, now that, with artificially low interest rates, the capacity of the individual to save for his old age is made more difficult!

This low interest rate policy puts the government in competition with all private lenders, forcing down interest rates all around—a leveling process affecting everyone.

There is a growing conviction among thoughtful people, however, that a society of personal and political freedom and a free enterprise market economy are integral parts of each other.

And it is just beginning to dawn on these same people that a free money market—one in which the interest rate performs its historic functions of determining where to invest, and governing the demand and supply of capital—is also an integral part of the free society.

Government spending and lending for housing, for agriculture, and for innumerable other purposes are all tied in with this further effort of leveling incomes.

8. Minimum wage legislation: Minimum wage law bars any worker from a job unless he can find an employer who is willing to pay at least 75 cents, $1, or whatever the fixed hourly rate may be. Whenever the minimum is raised, all the wage rates above the minimum also receive an upward thrust to maintain the historical differentials of the wage structure.

Minimum wage law has become a device for hoisting the whole general wage level. Here is another way of passing money from one group to another.

9. The labor movement: If one examines the President's economic reports and programs submitted to the Congress as

well as the several reports of the Council of Economic Advisers, one discerns a clear-cut policy of utilizing the labor movement to cut down the earnings from job-making to the benefit of the job-holder. While things are said on all sides of this complicated issue, again and again there is much talk of a deficiency of purchasing power. There is much discussion of encouraging wage increases (sometimes with the limitation "where they will not cause price increases").

While economists generally agree that deficiency of mass purchasing power is not the cause but the result of depressions, much pressure is generated in Washington in support of the unorthodox and generally unaccepted "underconsumption" theory of boom-bust which is so often utilized to justify the upward wage thrust.

By building up the labor movement through Wagner Acts and pulling the teeth of Taft-Hartley, the labor unions are encouraged to strive more aggressively for a larger slice of the national income. The employers are deprived of their natural resistance to encroachments by the unions. Extending the areas of collective bargaining to include numerous fringe and other benefits is another attempt to get for labor a larger and larger slice of the national pie. By reducing the prerogatives of management and enlarging labor's voice in management, the earnings of investors are steadily reduced.

As investors become more skeptical of future earnings and the security of investment, the way is paved for "government going into business" because, it is alleged, private capital won't come forth for investment.

10. Estate and inheritance taxes: What the government can't get during your lifetime the government can get when rigor mortis sets in and your executors begin to look over what's left.

There you have ten ways by which income is being equalized.

The processes of the rising American welfare state are now easily recognized. There is no direct action against them under our established political and social institutions.

Men and women who foresaw the end in the beginning, now nearly a generation ago, see little chance to stop short of the British, who traveled a similar road.

Socialism establishes its own need by forestalling the natural forces of capitalism. The mass of the people develop a psychosis of economic security which destroys independence, risk and ambition. The politician who is personally opposed to socialism seeks to stay in office by rationalizing that he should remain in power to temper the wilder ideas of the opposition. The middle class, the savers and investors, by their caution and fright create the very conditions which the Socialist then proceeds to cure.

Underneath it all is a two hundred year old struggle in America—a struggle for democracy to restrain itself against its own destruction.

THE LIBERTIES WE ARE LOSING [3]

Clearly disturbed by a rapidly growing apprehension among the people that the current Truman program points toward socialism and away from personal freedom, Administration orators, including the President, are resorting to an old trick known as a "poser." A poser in political usage is a question framed in such a manner as to allow either no answer at all or an answer favorable to the person who asks the question.

The current poser is: "What liberties are you losing?" The manifesto issued in Chicago by the Democratic National Resolutions Committee [4] puts the issue in affirmative form: "the achievements . . . in the past seventeen years" have been accomplished "without depriving one single American of one single liberty."

In reply, let us begin with a primary material liberty—the right to use personal income for purposes determined by the earner of that income. This liberty has been steadily, rapidly, alarmingly narrowed.

Twenty years ago, according to Herbert Hoover,[5] all units of our government were taking less than $200 annually from the average family. Today, government costs that family $1,300.

[3] From "What Liberties Are We Losing?" by Raymond Moley, columnist and author. *Newsweek.* 35:88, 92, 96, 96, 92. May 29, June 5, 12, 19, 26, 1950. Reprinted by permission.

[4] See "Program of the Democratic Party," in section on Merits of the Welfare State.

[5] See next selection, "The Last Mile to Collectivism."

The various programs now proposed would greatly raise the cost, perhaps by a third. Meanwhile, the number of people receiving government money has risen to something like 15 per cent of the population. If we add dependents, the figure will be two or three times as high. All these people are becoming increasingly dependent upon government. Their liberty is thus ebbing away.

The ratio of government expenditures to the total national income is moving upward. The percentage has not yet reached the 40 per cent figure of Britain, but it is in the mid-20s.

All this means that government has taken from the people more and more of their personal property and has determined how it should be distributed. Those in power, cynically hiding their purposes behind the good word "welfare," take the substance of all the people and return it to some of the people. Their assumption is that they know best. The liberty to have and to hold and to dispose of what is earned is vanishing.

And the program for the future set forth by the President and . . . the national committee is an ominous threat to contract still further the boundaries of personal economic liberty.

Ah, but a rich promise goes with this proposal to spend more. The gross national product will be increased to $350 billion. That may be true, but it is speculative. The proposals to spend more are not speculative.

The reality of taxation is never explained by these self-professed defenders of liberty. A farmer in Georgia, for instance, who believes he is getting something for nothing from the government, is not told what he pays for his benefits. The fact is that on one item, gasoline for his car, he pays 192 taxes. A similar mass of taxes is hidden in other things that he buys. Since the clear intention is to increase these taxes, the tide is running toward complete expropriation. That means socialism —nothing less. The disciples of Marx have always held that the most direct non-violent means to a Socialist state is through taxation. And there are no personal liberties under socialism.

Inflation is another means of curbing personal liberty. Savings have already suffered a tremendous shrinkage in real value. The prospect is terrifying. For if the program outlined by the

President and the national committee should be adopted, at least three quarters of the people's savings will be taken. That means that thrifty people who provided for their own future will have to fall back on the protective bounty of government. The man who wants to enjoy freedom to start a business will find little venture capital and must mortgage himself to government. Colleges and other free social and educational institutions will find fewer donors and will have to turn to government.

All these are among the material liberties we are losing. . . .

But the more the whole question of personal liberty is considered, the more it becomes apparent that property or material rights cannot be set off from non-material rights, such as worship, speech, petition, and assembly. The individual's inalienable rights are also inseparable. They depend upon each other and they are, moreover, equal in importance.

This principle of inalienable, inseparable, and equal rights was once firmly established after a long struggle to secure man's basic freedoms. It was established in the custom and fundamental law of free nations such as England, France, and the United States. The Constitution of the United States associates the three fundamental liberties: life, liberty, and property.

From John Locke onward, the essential nature of property was described as something of value which the individual had created by mingling his mental or physical effort with some material gift of nature in such a manner as to make it a personal attribute. It is the individual's because into its creation has passed some of his own personality. It stands on all fours with his rights to worship, speak, and otherwise express his thought and feeling. And it is limited only by the similar rights of other individuals.

Those who would quarrel with this definition on the ground that some property is inherited or received as a gift overlook two elements in such property. One is the fact that the right of the creator of such property involved his choice of its disposition. It is still private property. Another factor is the element of trusteeship, in which possessors of such property are bound by an obligation to those who have transmitted it. All this is embodied in our law and all of it is rooted in the basic tradition of our Constitution.

All this, however, is denied in the philosophy of the super-state and socialism. The Communist, of course, is perfectly frank in denying not only the individual's right of property, but all other rights. The Socialist has either less realism or less honesty. He argues, and I have heard Prime Minister Attlee expound on this at length, that while government may proscribe private property, it leaves all other rights in the individual. The citizen may lose his shirt, but he can still go to church, make speeches, and publish his opinions. His liberty is even enhanced, argues the Socialist, because, presumably, he has less responsibility to look after his property and can spend more time worshipping, speaking, writing, and petitioning.

The fallacy of this is shown in the financial predicament in which British socialism now finds itself. The cost of government has moved to prodigious heights, partly because government has been an inefficient operator of industry and partly because government beneficiaries have taken more than the government anticipated. The result is that the Socialist government is now moved to curtail rights. Labor unions are forbidden to quit work in strikes. In one instance, the government threatened action if a strike vote were held. Free medicine has become so expensive that government must, as its next step, tell the doctor whom he will serve and the citizen what doctor he may have. The essential indivisibility of rights has been demonstrated in every Socialist experiment. . . .

The American sponsors of super-statism have had a great deal of trouble getting around the constitutional guarantees of the rights of life, liberty, and property. For when these are joined in an indivisible triangle of liberty, they constitute our most powerful defense against the invasion of socialism. The one which they need to eliminate or breach, of course, is the right of property.

Three methods of attack have been used for this purpose in legislative and judicial action. The first is to break down the defenses of property through a wide, almost unlimited use of the general welfare clause in the Constitution. The second is to rate the three rights of life, liberty, and property in a descending order of importance. The third is to attempt to disassociate the right of property from the rights of life and liberty and to substitute for it a "right" of security.

The first two of these methods have found help and sympathy not only in the legislative declarations of Congress but in the Supreme Court as reconstructed over the past thirteen years. The third method, which is especially emphasized in the effort of the United Nations Commission on Human Rights, has reached the point of inclusion in the FEPC bill endorsed by President Truman and urged by his representatives in Congress.

The term "general welfare" appears twice in the Constitution. It is in the Preamble: "promote the general welfare," and in Article 1, Section 8: that Congress may tax to provide, among other things, for the "general welfare of the United States." Under an interpretation of the reconstituted Supreme Court, a great number of Federal grants, benefits, and regulations for all sorts of groups and purposes have been allowed. The point seems to have been forgotten by all but a minority of the Court that the words "general welfare" mean something more than the sum of all little welfares. For if enough little welfares are provided, the general welfare of the nation will be hopelessly impaired. But an opening has been made in the Constitution for almost anything a political Congress and President may find it expedient to provide.

Another trend has been a disposition of a group of Supreme Court Justices, notably Murphy, Rutledge, Black, and Douglas, to regard the three rights of life, liberty, and property in an order of descending importance. This tendency was vigorously resisted by the late Chief Justice Stone without avail. Justice Frankfurter has more recently protested about this "preferred position" of life and personal liberty, over property. This double standard has also been pointed out—not to say deplored—by the notable and respected Judge Learned Hand. He has very forcefully pointed out the truth that has been assumed for nearly a century and a half: that there is a strict equality of all three rights.

In defending the FEPC bill, Senator Lucas, the majority leader and presidential spokesman, asserted that the right of life was placed "above all others" and that life meant "livelihood" and that hence the FEPC bill should pass. This is utter confusion, of course, but it shows the trend of Fair Deal thinking. Property, therefore, becomes a third-class right.

Finally, there is the Universal Declaration of Human Rights of the United Nations, adopted a year and a half ago. This lists a whole flock of new "rights" and drops property to some vague language in Article 17. It revises the old trilogy of individual rights as follows: "Everyone has the right to life, liberty, and security of person.". . . .

While President Truman and his Fair Deal supporters have studiously avoided saying that they are seeking to put into effect a planned economy for the nation, if they succeed in electing a Congress that will enact their program, the fact is that we shall have an economy as planned as the British Socialists were able to achieve in five years of power. This can easily be shown by adding together the major items of the Fair Deal. . . .

Let us begin with compulsory health insurance. Here the government collects a tax, sets up the machinery for providing services, pays the doctors, directs patient participation, and foots the bills for all services, including drugs, hospitalization, eyeglasses, and so forth. The spurious claim is made that the patient may, among other things, select his doctor, and the doctor his patient. In practice, this choice would be very limited, and in the end, as Britain is learning, there could be no freedom of choice at all.

Innumerable proposals have been made to provide easy credit for small businesses through government loans. Careful analysis makes it plain that this plan to set up government-financed businesses in competition with privately financed businesses will strike at the very heart of a free economy. For it will support inefficient businesses and burden the efficient. And as one of its sponsors has admitted, much of the productive plant of the country will under foreclosure ultimately be owned by the government.

The current drive against bigness in business means telling enterprise how large it can be.

Tax exemption for cooperatives puts private enterprise at a deadly disadvantage against government-supported socialized enterprise.

The FEPC bill . . . places an obligation, under severe penalties, on a minority of employers to hire those the government decrees to be proper employees. It would deny some employers the liberty that it accords to others.

Administrative absolutism in many regulatory commissions and agencies has the effect of denying citizens access to the courts.

Repeal of the Taft-Hartley Act proposes to deny employers rights freely granted to and protected in labor unions.

The operation of a great federal political machine, with hundreds of thousands of jobholders and vast patronage, impairs free elections in every state.

The trend of pension and welfare legislation takes from the individual the responsibility and power of providing for himself.

The Brannan plan for agriculture pushes still farther a limitation upon the farmer in a free market. It penalizes larger farms. And in its provisions for perishables, it subsidizes every grocery basket at the taxpayer's expense and in effect tells the farmer what he shall receive for his product.

The most gigantic example of planning, however, is the proposal for a series of river valley authorities which would ultimately cover the nation. These are to follow the pattern of the TVA. The Columbia Valley administration is first on the list, and President Truman vigorously argued for it on his recent western trip. Under the Columbia plan, there would be three board members, virtually irremovable during a six-year term, with vast powers over electric-power production, navigation, irrigation, and many related activities. States would be denied their traditional control over their rivers, their land, and their resources generally. Local communities would be compelled to accept grants from the CVA in lieu of [revenue from] taxes. Almost every business and individual enterprise, from the small farm to the vast lumber industry, would be subjected through the control of electric energy. As a major spokesman for the plan has said: "He who controls electric power controls people."

These are a few of the aspects of the American grand plan. . . .

The prospect is enchanting. A tight little life with everybody equal. Hordes of officials peering into every corner of our lives. A barren plain of uniformity, over which ride the inspectors and police of a superstate. A fine end for a nation of once self-respecting pioneers! As Churchill once exclaimed in another connection: "What kind of people do they think we are?"

In 1947 Prime Minister Attlee admitted that seventeen ministries had the power to enter private houses without search warrants. That is the ultimate picture of a planned state.

But, says the planner, you still have freedom of thought and expression. Let us see. As freedom of choice ceases in the use of earnings, in occupation, in the things bought and sold, in caring for ourselves and our dependents, our minds lose the habits of freedom. The superstate hires a greater and greater number of us, and we learn that it is best to keep our mouths shut and our opinions to ourselves. The businessman whose customer is the government must realize that the customer is always right. Our private cultural, educational, and religious institutions, denied contributions from private savings, become government dependents.

In the end, there must be very little left for free expression and thought. Somebody else does all the thinking about everything important in life. Moral and intellectual atrophy sets in, and self-reliance evaporates in the thin air of absolutism.

The planning of things ends in the planning of men.

THE LAST MILE TO COLLECTIVISM [6]

We must wish to maintain a dynamic and progressive people. No nation can remain static and survive. But dynamic progress is not made with dynamite. And that dynamite today is the

[6] From text of address by former President Herbert C. Hoover on his seventy-fifth birthday, at Stanford University, California, August 10, 1949. New York Times. p3. August 11, 1949. Reprinted by permission.

geometrical increase in the spending of our governments—
Federal, state, municipal and county.

Perhaps I can visualize what that growth has been. Twenty
years ago all varieties of government, omitting federal debt
service, cost the average family less than $200 annually. Today,
also omitting the debt service, it costs an average family about
$1,300.

Now, that is bad enough. But beyond this is the alarming
fact that at this moment the executives and legislatures of our
country are seriously proposing projects which, if enacted, would
add one third more annually to our national spending. And if
you add these items to the debt service the average family will
be paying about $1,900 a year taxes. They might get a little of
it back if they live to be over sixty-five years of age.

Now no doubt life was simpler about 147 years ago when
our government got well under way. At that time there was
less than one government employee, federal, state and local,
including the paid military, to each 120 of the population. And
so late as twenty years ago, there was one government employee
to about every forty of the population. But, today, there is one
government employee to about every twenty-two of the population, and worse than this there is one government employee to
about eight of the working population of the United States. . . .

Twenty years ago, persons directly or indirectly receiving
monies from the government—that is, officials, and soldiers,
and sailors, and pensioners, and subsidized persons and employees of contractors working for the government—. . . represented about one person in every forty of the population.

Today about one person out of seven in the population is a
regular recipient of government monies. Now if all those of age
are married, they comprise about one half of the voting strength
of the last presidential election.

I would like for you to think that over.

In the long run it is the average working citizen who pays
through hidden and other taxes. And I've made up a little table
showing the number of days which this kind citizen must work
on an average in order to pay the cost of his government.

For obligations for former wars he would have to work eleven days a year; for the defense and cold war, twenty-four days more; other federal expenses another twelve days; for state and local expenditures fourteen days more, and that, so far, makes up a total of about sixty-one days out of each year.

But beyond this the seriously proposed further spending which is now in process will take another twenty days of work from Mr. and Mrs. Average Citizen.

Taking out the holidays and Sundays and average vacations, there are only about two hundred thirty-five working days in the year, and therefore a total of eighty-one days a years for taxes will amount to about one week in every month.

Now you might want to work for your family instead of paying for a gigantic bureaucracy. . . .

One end result of the actual and proposed spending and taxes to meet them is that government becomes the major source of credit and capital in the economic system. At best the small businessman is starved in the capital he can find. Venture capital to develop new ideas tends to become confined to the large corporations, and they grow bigger and bigger. Governments do not develop gadgets of improved living.

And another end result and one that should appeal to all of us is that it exposes our independent colleges and our other privately supported institutions to the risk of becoming dependent upon the state. Then through politics we will undermine that independence from which standards and stimuli to government-supported institutions must arise.

No nation grows stronger by such subtractions.

Now it's proposed that we can avoid these disasters by more government borrowing. That is a device to load our extravagance and waste on the next generation. But increasing government debts can carry an immediate punishment, for that is the road to inflation. There is far more courage in reducing our debts than in increasing them. And that is an immediate duty to our children.

And there's no room for this spending and taxes except to cut the standard of living of most of our people. Any way you can work it out it comes to that end. It is easy to say that we'll increase corporation taxes. But that's an illusion. The bulk of corporation taxes are passed on to the consumer—and that is to every family. It is easy to say to increase taxes on higher personal income brackets. But if all the incomes over $8,000 a year were confiscated it would cover less than 10 per cent of these actual and proposed spendings.

The real road is to reduce spending and waste and defer some desirable things for a while.

There are many absolute necessities; there are many less urgent meritorious and desirable things that every individual family in the nation would like to have but cannot afford. To spend for them or borrow money for them would endanger the family life and the family home. And so it is with the national family.

So long as we must support the necessary national defense and the cold war at a cost of twenty-four days' work per year to Mr. Average Citizen, there are many comforting things that should be deferred if we do not wish to go down this road to ruin in our national family life.

It merits thought from you.

We have a few hundred thousand Communists and their fellow travelers in this country. They cannot destroy this republic. They are a nuisance and require attention. We have doctrinaire Socialists who peacefully dream along about their utopia.

But there is a very considerable group of fuzzy-minded people who are engineering a compromise with all of these European infections. They fail to realize that our American system has grown away from the systems of Europe by two hundred fifty years. They have the foolish notion that a collectivist economy can at the same time preserve personal liberty and constitutional government. That cannot be done.

The steady lowering of the standard of living by this compromised collectivist system under the title of "austerity" in England ought to be a sufficient spectacle for the American people. They have aimed at the abundant life and wound up with a ration.

Now most Americans do not believe in these compromises with collectivism. But they do not realize that through governmental spending and taxes our nation is blissfully driving down a back road at top speed.

In the end these solutions of national problems by spending are always the same—power, more power, more centralization in the hands of the state. And along this road of spending the government either takes over, which is socialism, or dictates institutional and economic life, which is fascism.

We have not had great socialization of property, but we're on the last mile to collectivism through government collection and spending of the savings of the people.

You must give it thought.

And the device of these advocates of gigantic spending is the manipulation of words and phrases and slogans to convey new meanings different from those that we have long been used to. The malignant distortions drug our thinking. They drown it with emotion. For instance, we see government's borrowing and spending transformed into a soft phrase called "deficit spending." And the slogan of the "welfare state" that has emerged as a disguise for a totalitarian state by the exact route of spending.

And out of these slogans and phrases and new meanings of words come vague promises and misty mirages—we had the "security from the cradle to the grave." But in action these frustrate those basic human impulses to production which alone make a dynamic nation. . . .

The founding fathers dedicated the structure of our government "to secure the blessings of liberty for ourselves and our posterity." We of this generation inherited this previous blessing. Yet as spendthrifts we are on our way to rob posterity of its inheritance.

NO WELFARE WITHOUT SOLVENCY [7]

Opponents and critics who use the phrase "welfare state" are at a disadvantage. To attack it they are obliged to do so indirectly. "Welfare" as such can no more be successfully attacked

[7] From "Welfare State Faces Question: How to Make Security Secure," by Mark Sullivan, columnist and author. New York *Herald Tribune.* p21. October 28, 1949. Copyright, 1949, New York Herald Tribune, Inc. Reprinted by permission.

than sin can be defended. The objection to the welfare state is not to the welfare it purports to provide; it is to the regulation of the people that accompanies it, the deprivation of individual freedoms. Opponents seek to make the people see that the welfare state is likely to become the "slave state," the "serf state."

Without doubt there could be a great public debate and crystallizing of opinion on whether the people prefer to hold on to their individual freedoms, or give them up for the promise of welfare held out to them. . . . A direct way to raise the issue would be to examine the welfare which the Administration promises, to inquire whether the welfare that is promised could in fact be achieved and maintained. There is a real question here.

Much of the promised welfare consists of various forms of security—security for old age, the security of unemployment insurance, security in the form of various benefits, many sorts of security that are dependent upon payments to beneficiaries at some future time. The time when the security is made good may be far ahead—ten years or twenty or thirty.

All these securities rest upon one security, the security of the security. Will the beneficiary actually receive at the promised time, ten or twenty or thirty years from now, the security he is now promised? He will of course receive the number of dollars promised, $100 a month, or $50 or whatnot. But will those dollars, at that future time, give him as much real security as he is led to expect? To ask that is to ask whether the purchasing power of the dollar will remain what it now is, with no more than normal and immaterial change.

Here is a real issue vitally connected with the welfare state. It is timely right now. It can be worded as a question: Do the present policies of the Truman Administration—the welfare state and its policies generally, especially its fiscal policies—give confidence that the purchasing power of the dollar will remain stable over the years?

To that question many thoughtful persons answer that we cannot have such confidence if the Administration continues the present course of spending more than it takes in, a deficit last year, a larger one this year, a still larger one certain next year, future ones made almost certain by new promises and obligations to spend. If this course is not reversed, the consequence must be as Senator Byrd starkly puts it: "The government credit wrecked."

Here is a real issue. . . . It covers the welfare state but is broader, for the ultimate consequence of continued deficit spending would mean disaster not only to beneficiaries of government security programs but to everybody. To make this issue clear there must be patient education of the public; it is not enough merely to cry "welfare state" and "statism"—the terms must be explained. Men of careful thought must labor earnestly to explain an intricate and abstruse thing—just why it is that continued deficit spending, continued increase of the government debt, results in reducing the purchasing power of the dollar. The people must be shown that if deficit spending goes on indefinitely, the dollar would become in purchasing power, a half dollar, a quarter, a dime. They must be shown that, without solvency of the government, there can be no welfare state and no welfare at all, that there cannot be security for security.

TWO KINDS OF SUBSIDIES [8]

Subsidies fall into two major groups: those which are intended to accomplish some tangible undertaking, and those which are aimed at levelling incomes. The latter are a feature of the welfare state; the former are not. In recent months, there has been considerable confusion of the two types by writers . . . who attempt to trace the history of the welfare state in America back a century or so.

For example, the historian, Henry Steele Commager,[9] . . . points to railroad land grants and grants to settlers in the 1850s and 1860s as subsidies which constituted forerunners of the welfare state. Nothing could be further from the truth. As a matter of fact, land grants were made from motives which were largely just the opposite of the trend toward growing centralized government so characteristic of the welfare state.

There was a purpose behind the railroad land grants which had nothing to do with the welfare of individual companies or

[8] From "Subsidies and the Welfare State." *Economic Intelligence*, publication of the Economic Research Department, Chamber of Commerce of the United States. No. 22:1-20. May 1950. Reprinted by permission.
[9] See "A Long-Range American Development," in section on Merits of the Welfare State.

persons, although it did relate to "the general welfare" of the nation. The United States was faced with the problem of population concentration in the East and on a small strip of the West coast, with vast open spaces in between. It was apparent to military and civilian leaders alike that the West coast could not be maintained as a part of the United States without adequate rail communications to the East.

As General William T. Sherman said on one occasion, "The Northern Pacific must be built, both as an economic and military necessity. The West can never be settled, nor protected, without the railroad."

It was also apparent that no railroad could hope to operate over a thousand miles of empty country which originated no traffic without some offsetting advantage. Thus an incentive was provided in the form of land, for several reasons:

1. The Government had an embarrassment of riches in its land holdings. It cost the taxpayer nothing to give land subsidies.

2. Most of the land was not surveyed, and land values were so low that the cost of surveying it was far out of line. In Texas, where typical railroad grants were sixteen square-mile sections per mile of rail, it was customary for the railroads to give eight sections to surveyors as payment.

3. It was expected that the railroads would see to it that the land was settled, in order to increase traffic along their lines, thus accomplishing the purpose of filling the void between East and West. As every school child knows, this was done through railroad-stimulated immigration from Europe, and migration from the East.

There was a widespread feeling, at the time, that government had no business owning large quantities of land, and that it should be turned over, as quickly as possible, to private individuals who would put it to effective use. This was the purpose not only of the railroad grants but of the Homestead Act of 1862, in which the real criterion was whether the land would be put to use. Settlers were given five years to make a go of it, after which the land reverted to the Government if they were not successful, whereupon someone else could try.

This is in sharp contrast to the subsidies of the welfare state, whose goal is the levelling of incomes, taking from A to give to B. Farm subsidies, for example, are intended to raise farmers' incomes above what they might be if left to free market determination. Brannanism has as a further goal the supporting of consumer incomes by subsidies.

There was no element of the welfare state, or of socialism, in the land grants, whose purpose was much broader, involving defense, settlement of the interior, and the stimulation of private enterprise by farmers and industry. Likewise, today, it would be ridiculous to confuse defense subsidies for the maintenance of a merchant marine, or the growing of crops or production of minerals for which we are now critically dependent on foreign sources, with the class-angled, income-levelling subsidies of the welfare state.

HOW AMERICA IS BEING SOCIALIZED [10]

In the social science textbooks of a generation or so ago socialism would have been defined as a type of national economy in which the government owned the factories or the means of production. Today this would be a confusing oversimplification. Just as there are great differences in the capitalisms of England, France, prewar Germany and the United States, there are various forms of socialism, and American socialism has certain characteristics which are peculiar to the genius of our people, their political history and the form of our government. In this atomic and billion-dollar age, the technique of socialism has been modernized and rendered more subtle. There is the socialization of incomes under which the government takes a major share of your income and spends it for you and others. There is the socialization of economic decisions such as government planning, and thirdly, there is the classic type of socialism which means the actual taking over of property or assets. This type of socialism or nationalization may be the very last of a series of related acts

[10] From an article by Robert S. Byfield, member, New York Stock Exchange. *Commercial and Financial Chronicle.* 171:1201+. March 23, 1950. Reprinted by permission.

or moves. It may be the end rather than the beginning of a chain reaction.

The bottles with socialism in them have likewise acquired new and misleading labels. Among them are such well-known ones as "a planned society," "a managed economy" or "a directed economy." We must likewise distinguish between "front door" socialism which boldly walks in under its right name and "back door" socialism which walks in small steps up the rear stairs.

The "welfare state" is a new phrase for an old theory of government under which government officials assume responsibility for the material welfare of the people. Its most attractive sales argument is that it promises people "economic security." It removes from them the necessity of worrying about their personal financial problems. The best way to explain how people live under the "welfare state" is to think of all of us (except government officials) being told what to do, when to do it and how to do it. Having done as we were told, we will then receive food, shelter, clothing, medical care, etc., according to our age and needs, regardless of how much we have individually contributed to the total production. All we need to do, to insure our economic security, is to do as we are told and stay out of trouble with the people who give us our instructions.

In this connection I don't believe I could do better than quote from Senator Hubert Humphrey, [former] president of Americans for Democratic Action, who said in the course of a Town Meeting of the Air debate with Senator Brewster of Maine a couple of months ago that the welfare state comprised specifically:

Effective price supports for farmers.
School lunches.
Adequate social security.
Unemployment compensation.
Development of public health facilities.
Adequate distribution of medical services.
Soil conservation.
Development of rivers and harbors.
Cheap electrical power.
Minimum wages.
Slum clearance.
Low cost public housing. . . .

Senator Humphrey . . . sets forth a dozen or so of social targets as though they were glittering trinkets or presents to be plucked at will from a gigantic federal Christmas tree, just for the asking. But first, let me give you another definition, that of a very dismal word, economics. In the light of what has happened in the first half of the twentieth century, I would say that "Economics is the social science that tells you there is no such thing as a free lunch." Perhaps, speaking of food, the Senator's list may rightly be compared to the menu in a very swank restaurant where there are no prices opposite each item, or the balance sheet of a business that sets forth only the assets without the liabilities, or a beautiful, well furnished house with all the latest gadgets from air-conditioning to television, which you buy with gladness in your heart only to find out after you move in that the carrying charges on the mortgage, the taxes and the overhead make living in it unbearable.

Well, what is the price of the welfare state? The price is a socialized America. Have we got the resources to buy it? We are a rich nation, the richest in all history. If money or wealth were all that were needed, perhaps we could pay the bill, but the insidious part of the transaction is that mere wealth or productivity is only one component of the bill or invoice. There are many others and if the American people were given a bill of particulars on that score, I doubt they would be so keen upon buying the welfare state. . . .

Let us get on with our bill of particulars, item by item, in the catalogue of socialism:

1. One of the most immediate and obvious consequences of the welfare state is its irresistible bias toward inflation. It actually decreases production over a period of time because it creates nothing or produces nothing itself, but merely redistributes income. It is a give and take process. It gives to the poor and takes from the rich, gives to the sick and takes from the well, gives to the old and takes from the young, gives to the tenants and takes from the landlords. This is nothing new and has been tried from time to time since antiquity. Voltaire aptly said that it was a device for taking money out of one set of pockets and putting it into another. Kipling thought it was a machine to "rob selected Peter to pay collective Paul." Beyond

an attempt to equalize incomes or level down wealth it stifles
initiative for very obvious reasons, and its administrative costs
are heavy, having been estimated at 12 per cent to 15 per cent,
a kind of brokerage charge. Our British friends make no attempt
at concealing that a principal Socialist goal is "fair shares for all."

In a free voluntary society the incomes of people are dependent upon their relative contributions to production, but in a
welfare state these payments are based upon need rather than
earnings based on work done. As the welfare state grows it
increases the percentage of the income which is derived from
legislative action rather than [from] work accomplished. To put
it another way, it . . . can have no result other than the impair-
ment of the incentive to produce. In addition, the higher the
benefits the less the incentives of the beneficiary.

2. At this point it is necessary to observe that absolute
government control of, and the ability to manipulate, money
rates and the money market is an integral but concealed and
little understood part of the welfare state. In the old days . . . it
was possible to earn about 5 per cent from thrift, self-denial
or savings whether direct or through life insurance. Welfare
economics could not exist without artificially cheap money, which
in brief, among other things, reduces the earning power of
capital and helps transfer income from higher to lower brackets.
It makes it easier for the government to compete with private
lenders. It reduces voluntary saving in favor of compulsory
saving. It has led to the virtual control of the portfolios and
lending policies of the 15,000 banks in our commercial banking
system. It is a complicated subject and I shall not dwell long
upon it. Without cheap money Senator Humphrey's list would
melt away like snow in the summer sun.

3. Closely related to and also contributing to the bias of the
welfare state towards inflation is its espousal of intense social
pressures from all sides to achieve full employment or even over-
employment. The chief victim, of course, will be the purchasing
power of the dollar. The documentation for this viewpoint is
profuse and at hand. Marriner S. Eccles, Vice Chairman of the
Federal Reserve Board, in a recent letter to Senator Paul H.
Douglas said:

In making a cheap money market for the Treasury we cannot avoid making it for everybody. . . . The Federal Reserve becomes simply an engine of inflation.

But high taxes and low interest rates are not the only actuating forces of inflation. The powerful labor union monopolies created by the Federal Government are doing more than their share. Under conditions of full employment, unions, if not controlled, may be able to force up wages faster than engineers, inventors, chemists and managers can raise the output per manhour. If they do this, and recent painful experiences in the coal and other industries show that they are, either prices must rise sufficiently to offset labor costs or unemployment will increase. . . .

4. The bank account or income of every one of us has on the average already been garnisheed to the extent of about 31 cents on each dollar by government for its own expenses, some through direct taxes but mostly through indirect or hidden taxes on hundreds of items in the individual budget. Of the remaining 69 cents much is controlled or influenced by governmental intervention, as for example, the price of sugar or milk. Already then, to the extent of almost a third we have departed from a voluntary free society, economically speaking, and have given over control to the state. One of the immediate effects is the discouragement of saving by taxpayers in the higher brackets who in the past have provided the bulk of investment capital for our industrial growth. If long continued the scarcity of venture capital can have disastrous effects upon the vitality of our free enterprise system and already some unpleasant results are making themselves felt.

5. Of course, our bill of particulars would hardly be complete without mentioning the steps which the government has been taking for the welfare of the farmers. For a generation now we have had one farm price support policy after another and sooner or later they all fail. Only World War II bailed out the Treasury ten years ago; now surpluses are piling up again. The Commodity Credit Corporation has a borrowing power of $4.75 billion but needs $2 billion more and has asked Congress

for it.[11] It is possible that $6.5 billion may be tied up in farm price support operations before 1950 crops are all in. The scope of CCC's activities is staggering. . . .

There is no price tag on the Brannan plan but it might run to $3.5 to $4.5 billion or so. As welfare state statistics (or shall I say astronomy) go, this is not unbearably more than present plans cost taken by themselves, but the functioning of the plan would necessitate such a network of regimentation and controls that socialization of American agriculture, already fairly well advanced, would be greatly speeded up. Just a quick look will be convincing. Argus Research Corporation in a recent analysis points out that the farmer would be producing for the United States Treasury and not for the market. There would be no incentive for middlemen or speculators to store commodities, even temporarily, because fresh supplies would be coming on the market. Price would lose its function of equating supply and demand. Washington would be forced more than ever before to decide for the consumer what he is going to eat and for the farmer what he is going to produce. If the proposition is tried out in only a few commodities it overlooks the interplay of those commodities within our economy. If Brannan started with butter, say, the price drop would curtail the demand for lard and other fats and oils which in turn might force in hogs, which would bring down the price of pork and injure cattle growers and so on.

No wonder Allan B. Kline, President of the American Farm Bureau Federation, said last December, when speaking of over-subsidizing agriculture, "This is the road to stifled initiative, expanded regimentation and a pyramided government piled on the backs of those who do the work. . . ."

6. So far we have mentioned the direction, controls and regimentation which follow the welfare state—functional if you please—but now let's get on with a look at government in business, government in competition with the citizen, the taxpayer—actual nationalization. It may surprise you to learn from the Hoover Commission on Organization of the Executive Branch

[11] This additional authorization, approved by Congress, was signed by the President on June 28, 1950.—Editor.

of the Federal Government that the United States already owns or is interested in a hundred important business enterprises. These concerns engage directly or indirectly in lending money, guaranteeing loans and deposits, writing life insurance, the production, distribution and selling of electric power and fertilizers, operation of railways and ships and the smelting and sale of metals, including the CCC which we have previously mentioned. Over $20 billion is invested in these enterprises and there are commitments to supply $14 billion more. This is much more than the value of the British railways, electric undertakings, road transport, coal mines and other nationalized industries over there. In addition, the Federal Government guarantees directly or indirectly about $90 billion of deposits and mortgages and the life insurance written by government agencies approaches $40 billion.

Take electric power, though. Publicly owned plants now comprise 20 per cent of total generating capacity, about 11 million kilowatts at the end of 1948 against a total of 56 million. In 1930, private power comprised 94 per cent and public power only 6 per cent. The average citizen is almost wholly unaware of the extent and future portent of this steady but relentless encroachment on private enterprise. He thinks only of the TVA, but knows little of the grip which public power has on our Pacific Northwest with the proposed CVA hovering overhead. To him the Southwestern Power Administration, the Rural Electrification Administration, the Central Valley Project in California and the Colorado River Project are only names. Central Valley is mostly power and will ultimately cost $411 million. SPA isn't hay either and will finally take over $700 million of federal funds to complete. The REA co-ops have received or have been promised $2,375 million by Congress. These few items alone show that the United States Government, beginning with almost a single power plant at Muscle Shoals, Alabama, in 1930, has made enormous strides towards socializing the electric power industry.

Government is not hampered by conventional accounting. Government projects are wholly or largely tax free and regardless of how much the United States Treasury has had to borrow to build them they are not generally charged interest as an element of cost. Obviously, when government power moves into an area, private ownership must get out, be condemned or sell out. If the government was obliged to keep its books the way private industry does, there could be no such thing as the "cheap electrical power" to which Senator Humphrey refers. Senator Bridges of New Hampshire has said, "The TVA yardstick rates are a brazen fraud on the public, the taxpayer, the consumer and the investor." The General Accounting Office of the Federal Government in a 1945 letter to the Comptroller General of the United States hints at the same conclusion, though in far more sedate language. . . .

The extent to which the Federal Government is involved in lending, including lending on real estate, may be gauged by its huge investment of over $10.5 billion in this field. A mere mention of some of these activities may be enlightening. There is the RFC, whose loans to Waltham Watch, Lustron and Kaiser-Frazer have recently made the headlines, the Federal Housing Administration, the Federal National Mortgage Association, the Central Bank for Cooperatives and many others. I cannot catalog them here. Perhaps the following taken from a security circular of a financial firm commenting on the bright prospect of building material manufacturers will illustrate our feeling toward federal lending for housing purposes:

During fiscal 1949 the government spent $282 million supporting housing. This will grow to $1 billion in fiscal 1950 and over $1.3 billion in 1951. Most of this money is used to buy mortgages, many of them of a character too doubtful to find private purchasers. By lending a far larger proportion of the value than is permissible for any private agency the government makes possible a large volume of construction. Now it is pressing for a new law to extend the housing program to the middle income group for $2 billion more.

What does all the above mean? What does it all add up to? Has it an over-all pattern or thread running through it? In his book, entitled *On Our Way*, Mr. Roosevelt in referring to the depression of the 1930s insisted that it could be cured only by "a measured control of the economic structure." In the dispensing of welfare or the setting up of a welfare state the sin or evil which is to be eradicated is an alleged concentration of economic power. The imbalance is to be eliminated or alleviated by a redistribution or reallocation of wealth and/or income. Yet, if we are correct in our appraisal of the methodology of the welfare state it seeks to cure an unhealthy concentration of economic power by the greatest concentration of political power in our history. We think the cure to be worse than the disease because it inevitably will:

Destroy or dull the American traditions of individualism;

Undermine the independence of the American farmer and businessman;

Liquidate or at least seriously impair the vitality of state and local governments by usurping their powers and centering them in Washington.

This last named effect is perhaps the most dangerous and insidious of all. It comes gradually and in small steps. . . . The growing tendency of the Federal Government to usurp as large a measure of the taxing power as possible at the expense of the states is a case in point. If the states and municipalities for one reason or another, whether it is for education, construction of hospitals, building of roads and other purposes, are obliged to come hat in hand to Washington for grants in aid and other handouts, it is only a question of time before they will lose in part their identities and powers. One of the most effective methods open to the Federal Government is the creation of regional authorities like the TVA, CVA, the SPA and the MVA which eventually become more powerful than the states in which they operate and the municipalities which they serve. . . .

The result upon our particular type of governmental structure, with its elaborate and delicate checks and balances and its great dependence for proper functioning upon the capacity for tolerance, compromise and self-government of the American people, will be to create a political vacuum. State socialism must be the successor.

THE INDIVIDUAL AND HIS GOVERNMENT [12]

This whole nation was founded not only for the liberty of the nation, but it was founded to establish the liberty of the

[12] From an address by Senator Robert A. Taft of Ohio before the annual meeting of the Chamber of Commerce of the United States at Washington, D.C., May 1, 1950. Printed by permission.

individual, and for a hundred and sixty years our success has been based on the fact that we have maintained the liberty of the individual, the liberty of the individual to live his own life and think his own thoughts and speak his own thoughts, the liberty of the press, the liberty of the individual to go out and choose his own occupation, the liberty of the individual to start and run his own business as he thinks it ought to be run, as long as he does not interfere with the right of other people to do the same thing. It is the liberty of the individual in every field, in the field of knowledge, in the field of business, which has gradually built this country up to a point where today we stand at the head of all peoples in the originality and self-reliance of the people and the productivity of the people and in the development of the tremendous industrial machine which lies at the basis of our standard of living today. Liberty of the individual, therefore, has been the very basis of the liberty of a free people.

And in the whole contest today between totalitarianism and freedom, it is the dignity of the individual, the dignity and the self-expression of the individual, the sense of the importance of the individual soul which distinguishes us from the totalitarian government where the individual is nothing and the state is everything. The dignity of the individual is the very basis of Christianity itself. Today we see a dangerous attack upon that freedom and that dignity of the individual. I believe the dangers of the modern trend are so great that the time certainly has come when we must arouse people to the importance of retaining those characteristics of themselves, those characteristics of the nation, those characteristics of our great American system, which have succeeded today as no other system in the world has ever succeeded.

It seems strange indeed that, at this point of success, we should be seriously threatened with the forces which would destroy the basis of the system. Yet that is the threat we have to meet today. We have to meet, first, the direct attack of those who want to socialize the entire United States and the entire world, the direct attack of those who would socialize indusry. We have even in Congress two bills—the Murray Bill and the

Spence Bill which propose to give the Government the right to go into any business that it wants to go into. That means, of course, gradually, that every individual becomes an employee of the Federal Government, an employee of government. Certainly, then, his liberty and his power of self-expression, to a great extent, are subordinated to the interest and the direction of the all-powerful state. We have a direct movement to regulate every business operation in detail, as in the Spence Bill, to fix prices and fix wages and ration commodities, to bring the state right down to every individual business in the United States and tell the men how they must run those businesses, to tell every family what they shall eat, when they get up in the morning, and when they shall go to bed at night.

We have the proposal today to subordinate all agriculture to the control of the Federal Government, a plan which undertakes to guarantee the farmers a high price on condition that they limit their production of wheat and corn and hogs and beef and every other thing they raise, in accordance with the direction of a Federal bureau, a complete subordination of the individuality of every farmer and every farm to a totalitarian government.

We have the proposal of Universal Military Training, where at least for a year every boy is to be subjected to the direction and indoctrination of a Federal bureau. We have the proposal that the state undertake to furnish free all medical service and, of course, if they do that, to determine exactly what medical service every one of a hundred and fifty million people shall get, what kind of doctors they shall get, what kind of service they shall get, where they shall get it and when they shall get it, all to be subject again to the direction of a state bureau; depriving the family of its right to determine how they want their medical service and what kind of service they want. That is only a forerunner of all kinds of free services, such as they have in Great Britain.

The important thing is that these measures proposed are common throughout the world. They have spread steadily throughout the world. There was a time back in the nineteenth century when we had succeeded in making the idea of free government and the free individual a popular philosophical concept.

It dominated the world and everybody throughout all Europe and all the world admitted that the best way for the people to get ahead was a system of free government; even where they did not have it, it prevailed in the thoughts of the people. Then, gradually, the totalitarian theory has gained strength, the theory that only the government can determine what is good for the people, only the government can benefit them, only the government is able to have the expert knowledge and make the comprehensive plans and has the power to carry out those plans, which, according to this philosophy, are necessary for the welfare of the people; but with a complete destruction of the liberty of the individual, of the liberty of thought, of all liberties which, for so long, we have had prevail throughout the world and, certainly, have dominated this country up to today.

Secondly, we have a more insidious threat to individual freedom and the power and dignity of the individual soul. That is the tendency right among our own people to look to the government for assistance, to look to the government for guarantees, to look to the government for all of these free services which any particular group thinks that group ought to have. Every group is attempting today to get the government to give them protection, to guarantee them what they think they are entitled to. . . .

I say that, no matter how well the case of the different groups may be presented, it is still true that as a matter of human nature each of those groups is today seeking assistance from the Federal Government. No one of them is sufficiently, it seems to me, willing to stand on its own feet and simply fight out its own battle on the basis of its individual power and the persuasive power that it may exert on public opinion through its direct action and the presentation of its case.

I will start with businessmen. . . . Of course, there are an unlimited number of lobbies of businessmen and, while I find that all of them in general admit competition is a good thing, there are quite a few of them who would like to be protected, of course, against unfair competition; but they go a little further than that. You have the small businessmen who are very much concerned about the competition of the chain stores and who seek government . . . [action] to prevent the operation of chain stores.

I find that the big business people whom I deal with, while again they admit that competition is a good thing, certainly do feel that there is an inherent right for them to run their business at a profit and a certain inherent right to keep the prices at a point at which these profits will be returned.

Of course, business has joined in the general movement to limit the production of oil in the oil fields. And plenty of businessmen in the coal business supported the Guffey Coal Act to prevent, in effect, competition in the coal industry. We have plenty of businessmen today who are concerned with government undertaking to continue various foreign loans in order that their export business may be continued and perhaps may be more profitable than it otherwise would be. We have the general movement for protection against foreign imports. I myself fear very much the effect of the importation of foreign goods if it once develops to a great extent, with the low cost of labor abroad, and yet I find that most businessmen want the government to step in long before they are hurt in order that they may not have the severe competition which is an essential part of our system and which is necessary if they are going to continue to grow in the efficiency of their own operation. . . .

We have the home builders and real estate men opposing strongly any program which may conceivably—and only conceivably, I think—cut down the scope of their own operations, but, at the same time, insisting that the Federal Government come in and guarantee business loans up to 90 per cent of the value of the property—sometimes 100 per cent of their cost— in order that they may proceed with their particular business on a more profitable basis than they could have otherwise done.

Then we have the farmers. I think most of the farm organizations take a very reasonable and statesmanlike position, but more and more you have the idea prevailing that the government ought to guarantee parity prices to the farmer, assuming that parity prices are those prices that the farmer ought to get. I believe we ought to work in the direction of his getting parity prices. But the idea of the government's guaranteeing this goes beyond anything that we have ever had in the past in the farm field. . . .

What does it mean? It means that the government undertakes to guarantee that every man receive what he is entitled to in this great commonwealth of the United States. If you do it for the farmers, why not do it for everybody else? If you undertake to guarantee a man what he shall have, you have to, in the end, have an all-powerful government.

Perhaps you have almost a parallel of it in the demand of the labor people that every man be guaranteed a job. We had that proposed in the full employment bill of 1946, that the government should undertake to guarantee a job to every man. Well, every man ought to have a job, just as the farmer ought to have a parity price, but it does not follow—in fact, you take a fatal step when you go beyond that and say that the government shall guarantee, because that substitutes government action for the entire operation of a free system, the incentive to work, the reward for character and ability and hard work and genius, which our system has given and which has been . . . the key, . . . the basis of that system.

When we had up this guarantee-of-job business, I remember we found that the idea really came right from the Soviet constitution. Section 118 says:

Citizens of the USSR have the right to work; that is, the right to guaranteed employment and payment for their work in accordance with its quantity and quality. The right to work is insured by the Socialist organization of the national economy.

Of course Russia can guarantee the right to work because they can put the man to work anywhere they want to put him. If they cannot find a job for him in Russia, they can find one for him in Siberia, and they do.

You cannot possibly undertake in any field to give the government power to guarantee the individual even what he is entitled to, without giving the government complete power over his entire life and over the entire field in which that operation is.

You cannot guarantee him a job unless you give the government the right to go into business and create jobs. You cannot give him that guarantee unless the government is going to say what job he shall take and at what wages. You cannot guarantee parity to the farmers unless you are prepared to step in with a complete control of agriculture and tell the farmers how much in acreage of this or that they shall plant and how they shall operate their farms.

So this idea that has crept into the farm field is one which is not agreeable to the leading farmers. Yet more and more I see it reflected every day in the programs proposed, from the Brannan Plan right down to a lot of Brannan plan substitutes; there is the basic concept that the government must guarantee the farmer parity prices.

Of course, you have one other job if you ever undertake this field. You have to determine what a man is entitled to and that is not a very easy job. No man, as a rule, is entitled to what he thinks he is entitled to, and you have a tremendous job to settle that in the beginning. Our system is based on the general theory that a man gradually gets the job to which he is suited and entitled. He will get a reward for the work which he himself does, for the education he acquires, for the various qualities which qualify him for particular work. I do not say our system works perfectly. It does not. There is a lot of hardship in it. It works better in a small town, in a small plant, than it works in a tremendously industrialized community. The fact that it does not work quite so well in a big industrial community has led to the proposal that we throw it all away and, instead of having rewards determined simply by the operation of the system, by somebody giving a man a better job because he thinks he is a better man for the job, we shall substitute for that the decision by some federal bureau as to what a man is entitled to, what he is qualified for and what job he shall get. If you ever get to that point, you will have come to the end of the freedom of the individual, it seems to me, and you will have come to a completely totalitarian state. Yet you have lobbies both in agriculture and in labor to insist that the government undertake exactly that guarantee.

Take the FEPC plan. Surely, there should be no discrimination. Surely, a Negro should have just as much right to a job as any white man or any other person, but the particular method proposed is that the government should guarantee that right, the government shall go to every employer in the United States and determine motive, as to whether or not he was influenced in turning this man down by reason of the color of his skin or his race or his religion or his past national origin.

You bring the government down to every individual employer—two million of them—in this country, and you undertake to impose a government judgment in lieu of the freedom that that employer has had to exercise his own judgment.

Then you have the general demand now for simply free services to people from the government, particularly free services in medicine. You have organizations here in the labor field in particular demanding free maternity service, free medicine, free payment for disability, free wages while sick or while you think you are sick. They are demanding free payment to support children.

It is easy to push forward because we do give free education, we do give a certain amount of federal service and we are moving, it seems to me, toward a general federal old age pension, a place where it is peculiarly difficult, I must say, for anybody today to earn enough during his lifetime to provide even a reasonable living after sixty-five. Of course, this is going to get more and more expensive, because, if we all live to be a hundred, the government has to support us for thirty-five years.

The thing that impresses me in all these measures is the danger of direct operation of the government on the individual. I am for a lot of government policy that works in the direction of trying to achieve the goals of fair prices for agriculture, for instance, but the danger, as I see it, is the direct effect on the individual and the destruction of individual liberty. It is the direct operation of government in the control of business, in the attempt to run every man's business, the attempt to run every man's farm, the attempt to tell every family how they shall live and what services they shall get, the attempt to tell every man what job he shall get.

Those are the operations which seem to me to be peculiarly abhorrent and dangerous to the American system.

FAITH IN INDIVIDUAL MAN [13]

Our nation was founded as an experiment in human liberty. Its institutions largely reflected the belief of our founders that men had their origin and destiny in God; that they were endowed by Him with inalienable rights and had duties prescribed by moral law, and that human institutions ought primarily to help men to develop their God-given possibilities.

Our experiment succeeded well. Out of it came great richness—spiritual, intellectual and also material. What we did attracted world-wide attention and we were to others "liberty enlightening the world." Largely under the force of our example the restraints of despotism were loosened, and throughout the world men gained better opportunities to develop the worth and dignity of their persons. It was the great age of liberation, of true liberalism.

Then, around the beginning of the century, it seemed that a change occurred. We had to meet the hardest test of all, that of material prosperity. Our good society had borne such tempting material fruits that, to many, material things began to seem all important. Our practices became disconnected from the religious faith that had formed them, and many ignored their duty to fellow man.

This lapse was the more serious because, at this same time, scientific knowledge was making our society more complicated and interconnected; our population was becoming more dense and more urban, and business and labor were organizing into larger units. On top of that came a world war, a world-wide depression and a second world war. The combined result was that individuals became less self-reliant, feeling themselves tossed about by great cyclical waves. Many felt that security and social justice were dependent on the ordering of society by a strong central government. We have now gone far in that direction.

The trend toward the all-powerful government has been even more pronounced elsewhere. In Russia, the Communist Party

[13] From an article by John Foster Dulles, special State Department adviser, based on an address given before the American Political Science Association. *Freedom & Union.* 5:27-32. February 1950. Reprinted by permission.

seized control and, as a dictatorship of the proletariat, put on their spectacular experiment in a completely socialized state. Their leaders were fanatical and purposeful in a postwar world which had largely become a moral, economic and military vacuum.

Communist practices derive from irreligious beliefs. Orthodox communism denies the existence of God or of a moral law. It holds that individuals are soulless members of a social group. Their individual personality is unimportant. The material welfare of the group is all important.

Communists admit that there are non-material things—ideas —and that ideas can be potent. But, as put by Stalin, "the material world is primary and mind, thought, is secondary. . . . Hence the source of formation of the spiritual life of society should be sought . . . in the conditions of the material life of society." He concludes that "the strength and vitality of Marxism-Leninism lies in the fact that it does base its practical activity on the needs of the development of the material life of society" and relies upon that for "setting into motion broad masses of the people and mobilizing them and organizing them into a great army of the proletarian party, prepared to smash the reactionary forces" (*Dialectical and Historical Materialism,* 1938).

We in the United States cannot evade that challenge, for it is now hurled primarily at us. In Soviet eyes we are the arch reactionaries to be smashed by the masses, rallying to the Communist slogan: "Develop the material life of society."

What will be our response to this challenge? It catches us a little off balance, because of the historical developments I have mentioned. Shall we promise the masses that, from now on, we too will seek primarily to develop the material life of society? Or shall we respond with renewed efforts to show the worth of a society that puts spiritual development first?

The choice involves moral, not merely practical, factors. What is man's chief end here on earth? If, as Communists say, the goal is a mechanically perfect machine for the production and distribution of material things, then we might consider the arguments in favor of an all-powerful central government which would direct the living of the people and decide what is done with the products of their labor. That, however, would be to treat human life as little different from animal life and that, most Americans would think, is wrong and to be rejected as wrong.

Most Americans still have spiritual ideals. We want to be a society of individuals who love God and fellow man and who fear only God and not any other man; who work hard as a matter of duty and self-satisfaction, not compulsion; who gain security, not out of what government takes from them, but out of their ability and willingness voluntarily to earn and save; who are self-reliant, resourceful and adaptable to changing conditions and for whom life is not merely physical growth and enjoyment but intellectual and spiritual development.

But also we know that material conditions do have a bearing on spiritual development. A measure of insecurity can be a stimulant. But dread of insecurity is a depressant. Sordid and unhealthy living conditions, and illiteracy, stunt spiritual development.

Since private efforts alone cannot deal adequately with such problems, government should not be indifferent to them. There are many governmental compulsions that, all would agree, should be accepted to help improve the material conditions of our society. We have some of them and there are other public projects of national scope, like enlarged insurance against unemployment and old age (social security), that are generally acceptable. But also there is a point where increasing governmental compulsion produces diminishing spiritual returns.

Political scientists have not charted the precise location of that danger point. It is perhaps a shifting reef. But certain signs suggest that we are already near that danger.

Taxes come closest to being an objective test. Today federal income and estate taxes are highly graduated and at a near wartime peak and we still have wartime excise taxes. Economic conditions are favorable to big tax collections. Yet the federal income fails, by about $6 billion, to pay for what the Federal Government is now doing. And the impact of federal taxes on states and cities is such that they cannot raise the money needed, at present costs, to carry on adequately their accustomed functions. Governors and mayors come as beggars to the White House lawn.

Another danger sign is the increasing political attention paid to the assumed views of what the Communists contemptuously refer to as "masses." Some politicians seem to believe that there is here such a group, that it partakes only of materialism rather than what President Truman recently referred to as our "Christian heritage" and that, to get its votes, it is necessary to throw it raw political meat. That is a course which, once begun, is fraught with danger.

Another danger sign is a world current so strong that none are immune from its suction. In 1917 the Communist Party ruled nobody. Now Communists rule about one third of the human race and the end is not in sight. Never before have so few come so rapidly to rule so many. Such a world trend draws others to it unless positive precautions are taken.

It seems, then, that the time has come to "stop, look and listen" before embarking on vast new governmental projects for compelling an increase in material welfare. We should consider not merely whether the professed end is good, but what the process of getting there will do to people's character, if it involves more governmental compulsion and less personal responsibility. Also, we should consider whether there are not alternative ways of getting to the desired ends that have more of a voluntary, less of a compulsory character. . . .

You will recall that Jesus discussed men's need for food and drink and clothing. "All these things," he said, "do the nations of the world seek after; and your Father knoweth that ye have need of these things." "But seek ye first the Kingdom of God and His righteousness; and all these things shall be added unto you."

The American people have been deeply influenced by that Christian directive. They did not ignore worldly things, but for the most part they did not exalt them as primary. Indeed, at the beginning, our people accepted great material insecurity in order to get freedom to worship God in their own way and to develop in themselves and their children what they believed to be God-given spiritual possibilities.

Of course, our society was not all good—far from it. There is, and always was, vast room for improvement and no basis for complacency. There were always those who treated material things as of first, not secondary, importance and, as we have pointed out, material selfishness at times led to much social injustice.

But our lapses have not been so grave or so prolonged as to justify sentencing the American people to shrivel, spiritually, under a paternalistic form of government.

Neither faith, reason nor experience warrants the conclusion that, in the case of a people as religious and as educated as are the American people generally, public materialism is the way to counteract the ills of some private materialism. There is no reason to abandon faith in the great American experiment, and every reason for resuming it.

That doesn't mean going back or standing still. The American people have been the most creative people in history. They are constantly pulling things down in order to put up something new and better. Their restless habits in that respect amaze people elsewhere. They have, to be sure, been kept under wraps in recent years. But their spirit is still vibrant and to say that the American people, unless spurred by government, will keep in the same place is to be more nonsensical than Alice's Red Queen.

Of course, it is impossible to do today, on a private basis, all that should be done. More than ever before in our peacetime history, government must be the means by which people cooperate. But that very fact makes it the more necessary to be selective and to stop assuming that whenever there is a social problem the way to solve it is to increase still more the power, the responsibility and the taxes of the Federal Government. And those who want freedom can and should put energy, resourcefulness, devotion and enthusiasm into finding solutions that will be voluntary and not compulsory.

The great need of our time is to recapture faith in the infinite possibilities of the individual human being and to translate that faith into works. That is the way, the only way, to surmount the grave perils, domestic and foreign, that confront our nation. . . .

Having been in the United States Senate, I can sympathize with the viewpoint of those who see a human need which apparently they can remedy if only they use increasingly their power to tax. In any individual situation the case for government action is powerful. But it must be remembered that the multiplication of such acts will make taxes so heavy as virtually to deprive all of our citizenry of responsibility and, as Justice Brandeis warned: "Experience should teach us to be most on our guard to protect liberty when the government's purposes are beneficent." In these matters, as in most others, dispute relates to methods not ends.

Those in power usually believe that the way to get good ends is to increase their power. They lose faith in the capacity and willingness of private persons and state and local authorities. They have complete faith in their own benevolence and in their own ability to withstand the corrupting influence of power.

Our founders had no such faith. They took great precautions to erect barriers against what George Washington, in his Farewell Address, referred to as "the spirit of encroachment" which ". . . tends to consolidate the power of all the departments in one, and thus to create, whatever the form of government, a real despotism."

They carefully restricted the powers of the Federal Government and stipulated that all others "are reserved to the states respectively, or to the people." But, in fact, the power of the states and of the people exists only on paper, if those in Washington lose faith in all except themselves, and, through taxes, monopolize the means of promoting the general welfare. . . .

For a century and more the United States was a materially weak nation. We had virtually no military establishment, and we were largely dependent upon economic help from others. Never, however, were we in serious external danger because we were strong in faith and dynamically espoused the cause of human freedom. What we did, caught the imagination of men everywhere, and no leaders, however personally hostile or ambitious, could have brought their people to try to crush out the great American experiment because that experiment carried the hopes and aspirations of all the peoples of the world.

We are in the process of losing that protection and because of that we are in great peril. A people are doomed if they think only of security and not of mission; if they seek safety in steel and not in the sword of the spirit. Our future greatness and our power lie, not in aping the methods of Soviet Communism; not in trying to contain them—and us—within walls of steel, but in demonstrating, contrastingly and startlingly, the infinitely greater worth of practices that derive from a spiritual view of the nature of man.

MEN INTOXICATED WITH POWER [14]

The people who settled this country did not come here to establish a government. They came to America to escape the tyrannies of government. They were seeking liberty, not security. They were seeking an opportunity to enjoy freedom, the freedom of being let alone.

They believed that every human being possessed certain inherent and inalienable rights by the grace of God and not by the grant of any government. To secure those rights, the people were willing to endure hardships and, if necessary, sacrifice their lives.

It is not surprising that when their numbers increased and it became necessary to establish some form of government, they grudgingly yielded powers even to local governments. They realized that if an individual lost his freedom, to him it was not material whether it was taken from him by an individual despot or by a temporary majority. History had shown that despots at times were beneficent, but mobs always were cruel.

When in due time the necessity arose for a union of the states for the common defense, they carefully weighed every word of the drafted instrument. They adopted a Constitution granting limited powers to the Federal Government, and specifically reserved all other powers "to the states, respectively, or the people."

[14] From an address by the Honorable James F. Byrnes, former Secretary of State, at the Conference of Southern Governors, Biloxi, Mississippi, November 21, 1949. *Vital Speeches of the Day.* 16:98-102. December 1, 1949. Reprinted by permission.

Then in the Bill of Rights they specifically prohibited the Federal Government interfering with the people's rights. . . .

But today is another day. . . . We are threatened with the concentration in Washington of the powers of local governments, including police powers, and with the imposition of creeping, but ever advancing, socialistic programs. To pay for these costly programs we are going to borrow more money. It is well to remember that if we but stumble there is no lend-lease or Marshall aid for us. We will be all on our own. . . .

Many people are disturbed. But those who look with fear upon the trend of political thinking, may as well be realistic. They should realize that if a proposal for the spending of money is authorized by the Congress as promoting the general welfare, the probability is that under the decisions interpreting the general welfare clause of the Constitution, it will be sustained by the [Supreme] Court.

Therefore, those who wish to preserve people's rights and prevent the gradual absorption of local governments by a big government in Washington, with resulting restrictions upon our liberties, should look to the people.

It will serve no useful purpose to argue to them about the repeal of federal aid laws which are in operation and to which operation the states have adjusted their budgets. Nearly 40 per cent of all money spent by the states comes from the federal treasury as grants in aid. The people are not apt to repeal these laws. But we can oppose their expansion until our budget permits it. And we can oppose the adoption of new and costly programs that other governments have tried and now wish to abandon.

It will serve no useful purpose to spend one's time in critizing the political parties or individuals responsible for the growth of the federal aid system. No party or individual is entitled to a monopoly of the blame or credit.

Among the advocates of big governments there are some who honestly believe that local governments have failed to discharge their responsibilities. The failure of state governments to provide more efficient government, is generally due to the fact that the

Federal Government has stepped in and monopolized most sources of taxation.

The governors of the states are conscious of the responsibilities, as well as the rights, of the states. If Congress will withdraw from fields of taxation traditionally regarded as within the jurisdiction of the states, the governors will have the states provide essential services at less cost to the people and less restriction upon them.

There is another group: Those people who feel that government must play a greater role and yet are opposed to a government doing everything. They do not know where the dividing line should be. To them I suggest that government should stop doing for people those things the people can do for themselves, or which can be done by local governments.

There is still another group—a dangerous group. They are the selfish men who love power—the power to spend the money of other people. They are in every department and agency and they want to stay there, but they are interested not only in a job; they love power. The bigger the government, the more money they have to spend and the more power they have.

We would not have an ever-expanding government if the people were conscious of the taxes they are paying to the Federal Government. When the government required employers to withhold income taxes from employees, the government put the worker to sleep.

Ask any wage earner the amount of the wage he earns and he will tell you the amount he receives in his envelope or pay check, and not the amount his employer actually pays for his services before taxes are deducted for the Federal Government.

The excise taxes are so well hidden that their burden is not appreciated by the average taxpayer. Not realizing that they are paying the bill, they are easily misled into clamoring for more federal laws and more federal aids. They are misled into regarding the United States Treasury as a Christmas tree with the President and the members of Congress playing the role of Santa Claus.

In the last fiscal year in peacetime the Federal Government collected $38 billion in taxes. The government did not live within its income. We spent $40 billion and had to borrow $2 billion to pay our current bills.

We are continuing to spend more than our income. . . . If Congress adopts . . . new programs no man can tell exactly how much we will have to borrow, or from whom we will borrow it. We do know the next generation must pay for it. All of us should think more of the next generation and less of the next election.

What a heritage we will bequeath to the children of this day! Our greed for welfare and security will deny to them the opportunities we enjoy. Instead of fighting freely for the future of their children, they will be forced to pay for the folly of their fathers. . . .

Big government is growing bigger. Big government is more dangerous than big business. Little governments can regulate big business and the United States government can punish those who violate the laws against monopoly, but it is difficult to regulate big government.

The spenders, while deploring deficit spending, assert as an excuse that there was deficit spending during the Roosevelt Administration. That would not necessarily make it right. But who can forget that in 1933 the banks of the nation were closed, farmers whose mortgages were foreclosed were deserting the farms, factories were idle and the unemployed walked the streets hungry?

Only a spender with no sense of responsibility could fail to see the difference. Today the banks have more money on deposit than ever before in peacetime history. Farmers are reasonably prosperous. Few factories are idle. More men are employed than ever before and the people are better fed and better clothed. It is rightly said we have "unexampled prosperity." If our government cannot now live within its income, what will it do should we have a serious recession in business?

Today our public debt amounts to more than a quarter of a trillion dollars. Yes, I said TRILLION! Daily we are adding to that debt. The interest on the debt is 5.5 billion, which is more than all expenditures of government were in 1933.

Should we have a depression and the people find it burdensome to pay taxes for the $5 billion interest, we may hear the demand that the government substitute for the outstanding bonds, the greenbacks of the government that bear no interest. We heard it in 1933. Should we yield to that demand, it would be the beginning of the end.

To justify spending more than our income, some persons speak of what the government is doing for the "little fellow." Let me show you what the Federal Government is doing *to* the little fellow. The United States Government is making the small man smaller every day.

If the "little fellow" sends a message by telephone or telegraph he pays a tax. If he travels by railroad or bus he pays a tax. If he buys an automobile, the sale price includes a tax. When he buys gasoline or oil he pays a tax. If he buys cigarettes, he pays a tax. If he goes to a football game or baseball game, he pays a tax. If his wife buys a pocketbook or cosmetics, she pays a tax, and if his children go to a movie, they pay a tax.

The average working man must work forty-seven days a year to earn the money necessary to pay his taxes to the Federal Government. That is almost one day out of every week. If the new programs now seriously proposed should be adopted he will have to pay in taxes the equivalent of his wages for an additional twenty days, making sixty-seven days he will work each year for the government instead of for himself and his family. That is what the Federal Government is doing *to* the little fellow.

If the spenders really want to help the little fellow, they should allow him to keep more of the money he gets for his labor to spend as he pleases, instead of having it taken from him and sent to Washington, to let bureaucrats spend as they think it should please him.

Men intoxicated with power will never voluntarily surrender the power to spend the money of other people.

PATERNALISTS VS. "ORIGINAL" LIBERALS [15]

The original liberal was a man who believed above all things in freedom for himself and for others. He believed particularly

[15] From "Liberalism, What and Where Is it?" by Donald R. Richberg, attorney and former government official. Founder's Day address at the American University, Washington, D.C., February 24, 1949. *Vital Speeches of the Day.* 15:327-9. March 15, 1949. Reprinted by permission.

in individual freedom from all unnecessary government restrictions. The modernized liberal believes above all things in freedom for a strong government to liberalize and to angelicize weak human beings with all necessary restrictions on their personal conduct and activities.

The original liberal wanted to preserve your right to make and spend your own money, and other ancient rights of free enterprise, free speech and free association. The modernized liberal is most notably liberal in spending your money for you and in giving away your rights to control your own business and social relations.

The original liberal thought that a man should be free to make enough money to provide, for himself and his dependents, insurance against the hazards of accident, disease, unemployment and old age. The modernized liberal thinks that the government should tax away your surplus earnings, and with this money provide insurance for you and your dependents, and for anyone else who doesn't earn enough to pay for his own insurance.

Please do not think that I am scoffing at these modernized liberals. These humanitarians are far more admirable citizens and better neighbors than those greedy money makers who destroyed the freedom of private enterprises by operating them with a ruthless disregard for the welfare of their fellow men.

But I do scoff, as an amateur scientist, at the deception practiced when a humanitarian who is a paternalist calls himself a liberal. These miscalled liberals are promoting a paternal government that is to make sure that all its children are employed and properly housed and fed and have no fear of want, a paternal government that collects a large share of the earnings of its children so that Uncle Sam can provide them with insurance against all hardships, and can pay an army of public employees to watch over them and make them happy and virtuous.

These men are not liberals in any true meaning of that word. They are paternalists who call themselves liberals because they know that the American people are not yet reconciled to a paternal control of their lives. They know that the American people still cherish the illusion that they can remain free men and yet be protected by government from all the burdens and hazards that a free man must assume.

So the politician who is engaged in taking away your freedom disguises his thought and purpose by announcing that he is going to set you free from fear and want and insecurity and injustice. A program to set you free would seem to be a "liberal" program. Yet it might be noted that the best example of such freedom from the burdens and worries of self-support which is provided by government today is found in government prisons, which are not called liberal institutions.

Again I beg of you to understand that I am not arguing that a modern government should not accept some responsibility for the economic welfare of its citizens, in addition to its long accepted responsibilities for public health and safety. That which is called a "welfare state" is the obvious modern successor to what may be called the "protective state" of past decades. The protection of society now calls for more than protection against foreign oppression and domestic disorder and crime and pestilence. It calls for more than merely laying down the rules of fair play in a free competitive economy. This will be generally conceded.

But there is a fundamental division of thought in our country on two major political issues. First, to what extent and at what speed should government undertake to eliminate social and economic injustices and provide economic security? Second, is the national government the most competent or desirable instrument of social and economic progress, or should state and local governments be utilized, wherever possible, to do the job?

There is a natural affiliation between paternalists who believe in extensive and rapid reforms and the federalists who would have all welfare laws enacted and administered by the national government. There can be little doubt that the national government, with its command of huge revenues and its remoteness from the pressures of local interests and prejudices can enact and enforce regulatory laws, against minority opposition with greater speed and often with more efficiency and less partiality than local governments.

On the other hand those who advocate more gradual reforms know that local government will not usually act except under the pressure of a local majority opinion. Thus there will be the sanction of prevailing opinion for a political experiment, and the opportunity for a prompt revision if the experiment should prove unwise. When we observe the continual adjustment and readjustment of state and municipal laws to meet changing conditions and changing public sentiment, in contrast to the slow and difficult process of revising any major federal law, we can see many strong arguments in favor of local self-government. State government, in regulating the liquor traffic and labor relations, has demonstrated a flexibility in response to public opinion which has been notoriously lacking in the national government.

There is, however, a more profound reason for maintaining the authority of local governments against the constant pressure to extend the authority of the national government. The impossibility of retaining a democratic control of a centralized government of a hundred and fifty million people is being demonstrated not only in America but throughout the world. Particularly, it has been made evident that the regulation of the daily living and working conditions of millions of people is only practical through the issuance of volumes of bureaucratic regulations to be applied by a multitude of petty officials, whose speedy and necessarily arbitrary decisions must be enforced by the hurried prosecution and harsh punishment of offenders. The traditional protections of the individual against abuses of official authority, which we call "due process of law," cannot be maintained. In a word, a comprehensive welfare state must be a police state.

It was one of the fundamental principles of our constitutional government that the police power—that general authority to protect and to promote the public health, safety, morals and welfare—should be reserved to the states. No such power was granted to the Federal Government. Such paternalistic controls over our citizens as become necessary must be exercised by local governments, which, being close to the people, can be readily restrained from interfering unduly with their individual freedom to pursue happiness according to their individual ambitions and abilites.

There is and always should be a deep-seated conflict of opinion between liberals, who believe in maintaining individual freedom by strengthening our powers of local self-government, and paternalists, who believe in hastening social reforms by increasing the powers of the centralized, national government.

PRACTICAL ALTERNATIVE: WELFARE ON A SELF-RELIANT BASIS [16]

The idea of the welfare state is becoming part of the air we breathe. Individuals may denounce it in the abstract, but when it comes down to specific cases—a crop support, a postal subsidy, a pension, a grant in aid for a scholarship—practically everyone finds a personal rationalization for taking from the state when and where he can. Since the drift of history is in the direction of the welfare state, it may appear utterly quixotic to stand in the way of a seemingly ineluctable fate.

Nevertheless, we persist in taking the risks of quixotry. We recognize all of the seemingly inevitable compulsions that have caused people to think they can get an absolute guarantee of security from government. Any guarantee of security that pretends to be absolute is, of course, a delusion. But insofar as security can be had, we insist there is a practical alternative to the welfare state that is worth wide popular discussion. We insist that history might go off on a new and creative tangent if people were only minded to pause and think the alternative over for a bit.

The practical alternative to the welfare state is not something called laissez faire, or rugged individualism, or any of the other pejorative phrases for capitalism. We would be tempted to call the alternative the welfare society if we didn't distrust the obsessive connotations which the word "welfare" has come to have. Insofar as security must be one objective of the good society (other and more important objectives are productivity, excellence, creativeness, adventure, honor, and the chance to take a chance) our practical alternative to the welfare state would con-

[16] "There Is Another Way!"—an editorial. *Life.* 28:34. March 27, 1950. Copyright Time Inc. Reprinted by permission.

cern itself with many welfare devices. In our preferred type of
society the means to security would be reliance, not on government, but on organizations promoted by the people themselves.
In our society people would predominantly prefer to experiment
with their own forms of association for mutual aid.

Seeking health, the people would not run to government for
medical aid. Instead, they would turn to Blue Shield and Blue
Cross and similar medical insurance societies. In the interests of
freedom, the well-to-do would willingly pay a higher Blue Cross
rate than those in the low income brackets. Doctors would practice "group medicine," pooling their mechanical facilities for
diagnosis (always an expensive item for the individual) and
working out fee schedules that would allow low income families
to join Blue Cross societies for a nominal sum.

Our society would encourage cheap housing. It would not,
however, put its reliance on government to get it. In a self-
reliant society, labor unions, for example, would use their treasury surpluses to enable their members to get housing money at
low interest rates. Unions would buy tracts of unimproved land
and pass individual plots along to members without charging a
subdivider's fee. Middle-class people who want homes would
enroll in building and loan societies. They would save their
money and lend it back to themselves at a low interest rate. They
would study the history of housing in Great Britain, where the
building societies staged a terrific housing boom in the 1930s
without government help.

In our society monopolistic prices would cease to exist. They
would be progressively undercut and eliminated by consumer
cooperatives, of which there would be a steadily increasing number. The potentialities of such a movement have already been
demonstrated in the Scandinavian countries, where the cooperatives not only sell to their members at prices close to cost but
also go into manufacturing many articles for themselves.

Social security must be one objective of any society in which
the aged are expected to retire. In our society people would get
security by establishing either industry-wide or regional nongovernmental public corporations, with public-spirited citizens of

wide business experience and proven competence functioning as
directors. The public social security corporation would invest its
capital in industry on a "balanced fund" basis—one third of the
money in bonds, one third in preferred stocks, one third in high-
grade common stocks. By following this method, the social
security corporation would plow the people's funds back into
production—and the production, in turn, would provide for real
security.

We are not suggesting here that government has no role to
play in helping people. Such things as education, road building,
flood control and soil conservation, since they involve a general
welfare that cannot always be promoted on a large and efficient
scale by voluntary private organizations, must involve some measure of governmental action. But even in these areas there could
be more, rather than less, reliance on voluntary organization.
People in rural areas have been helping themselves for years by
establishing voluntary conservation districts. There are even instances of nongovernmental river control projects—the Muskin-
gum (Ohio) Watershed Conservancy District is one such instance.

In following us on our little voyage to an imaginary country
it will have occurred to readers that we have not been projecting
a series of utopian hopes; we have merely been describing what
some people are doing already. We have merely been listing a
number of specific voluntary welfare mechanisms that have already proved themselves in practice. Private pension plans, Blue
Cross and Blue Shield medical insurance, housing societies, consumer cooperatives, public corporations and voluntary soil conservation districts are old stories. They are success stories, too.
And that is precisely our point: welfare on a self-reliant basis is
not a vague utopian hope but a very practicable possibility.
People can have it if they want it. We are sure that they would
want it in increasing numbers if they stopped to think it over.

THE WELFARE STATE ABROAD

EDITOR'S INTRODUCTION

In discussing the welfare state in the United States, both its defenders and its opponents look abroad for examples to support their views. Britain, in particular, is both pointed to with pride and viewed with alarm as an exhibit of the welfare state in action. Most discussed is Britain's all-inclusive national health service. Whether it is a comprehensive success or a complete fiasco depends upon who tells the story. The British Labor government, since its election in 1945, has nationalized the Bank of England, the coal industry, civil aviation, electricity, railways and overseas communications. Its efforts to nationalize the steel industry have been deterred, at least temporarily, because of the shaky majority which Labor obtained in the February 1950 general election. In addition, the Labor government has carried out a full employment program (with accompanying manpower controls), and has gone far in the field of government-supported housing and education. Food subsidies, along with a war-born rationing system, are part of Britain's welfare state. Another Reference Shelf volume [1] treats the British welfare state in detail.

In the section which follows, the Scandinavian and Australasian welfare-state experiences are examined, preceded by an overview of a welfare state of another day—that of Germany under Bismarck. This by no means exhausts the study of the welfare state abroad. The totalitarian countries, for example, are classified by some people as welfare states—but such a study is hardly within the scope of this volume.

BISMARCK'S WELFARE STATE [2]

It is worth while to examine the first great welfare state experiment. It was made in Germany by Bismarck seventy years

---

[1] British Socialism Today, by Julia E. Johnsen. Reference Shelf Series, vol. 22, no. 1, 1950. See especially pages 58-130.
[2] From an article by Sidney B. Fay, professor emeritus of history, Harvard University. *Current History.* 18:1-7. January 1950. Reprinted by permission.

ago. His social insurance against sickness, accident, old age, and disability was soon regarded by most people as highly successful. It had a strong influence a quarter of a century later upon Lloyd George when he introduced social insurance into Britain in 1911, and it gave an impetus to similar social legislation in many other countries.

Many things in connection with Bismarck's social insurance program seem paradoxical or unexpected. Why was it, for instance, that social security originated first in a conservative, strongly monarchical, almost semifeudal state like Germany rather than in a more liberal and more advanced industrial country like Britain? One reason is that Prussia had a strong tradition of paternalistic, monarchical care for the welfare of its population since the days of the Great Elector and Frederick the Great. Furthermore, Bismarck enjoyed sufficient authority in the Prussian-German state to push through social legislation when he finally decided that there was need for it.

This need, Bismarck believed, lay in the early and vigorous growth of a revolutionary, anti-government, political party—the Social Democrats. As early as 1880 he decided that their power and influence must be broken, not merely by negative, repressive measures but also by positive, social welfare legislation which would win their goodwill and support. In Britain, on the other hand, a Socialist (or Labor) party developed much later and was much weaker than in Germany. It was of little concern to the government until after the turn of the century. In Britain, moreover, the workers' interests were mainly taken care of by the trade unions which were relatively conservative. But in Germany trade unions were a relatively late development as compared with Britain and their influence was less. The German worker of Bismarck's day looked for backing and support to the Social Democratic party instead of to the trade unions.

It is also curious that the German social insurance laws were proposed and carried through by conservative groups in the face of vociferous opposition by the liberals, progressives, and Socialists.

But within a decade after Bismarck's dismissal in 1890 roles were reversed. After 1900 Progressives and Social Democrats usually favored further social security legislation. After World

War I they extended "security" measures to a dangerous degree, while the conservatives were helpless to prevent social welfare policies of which they disapproved.

Bismarck's own motives and changes of attitude were no less remarkable. His early social ideas were strongly conservative because of his religious feelings and his class position in the Prussian landed nobility. Later, in the 1850s he was much impressed by Napoleon III's social policies which were calculated to strengthen the Emperor's power and make the French masses contented: universal suffrage, recognition of workingmen's organizations, public works, rise in wages, housing, state-aided sickness insurance, and savings institutions for small depositors. All these measures did actually seem to strengthen Napoleon's position and gain for him the support of the masses to offset the criticism of the liberal middle and upper classes. Bismarck likewise, after becoming Minister-President in Prussia in 1862, proposed some measures of a similiar kind. But he was not yet strong enough, or perhaps not persistent enough, to get them adopted.

Ferdinand Lassalle's influence on Bismarck at this time was considerable. Bismarck rejected Lassalle's project for state-financed cooperative enterprises, but he did adopt equal, universal, male suffrage, as advocated by Lassalle, as the basis for elections to the German Reichstag. Today we would regard such an extension of the suffrage as a concession to liberalism. But in those days, in Bismarck's mind, as in Napoleon III's, universal suffrage was reckoned as a means for strengthening conservative monarchy by the support of easily led masses against the liberal bourgeoisie. But time often brings remarkable changes of attitude. A quarter of a century later, in 1890, when the German industrial masses, no longer docile, voted for Socialist deputies to the Reichstag and attacked Bismarck's policies, Bismarck seriously considered restricting the suffrage—by a coup d'état if necessary.

During the wars of 1864, 1866, and 1870 and the consolidation of the new empire in the following ten years, Bismarck was too busy, as he himself said, to give any thought to social legislation. It was not until 1878 that he became seriously concerned over the danger to the state from the Socialists. They had steadily increased their popular vote. Their representatives in the Reichstag voted against all his measures for consolidating the new empire. Their speeches and propaganda advocated the Marxian doctrines of social revolution and the overthrow of the capitalist state.

In 1878 two attempts were made on the life of old Emperor William by two mentally unbalanced young men. They were not indeed members of the Social Democratic Party, but Bismarck used their revolver shots as a justification for introducing a severely repressive bill against the Social Democrats and all subversive agitation. It provided for the suppression of Socialist meetings and newspapers and the arrest or expulsion of Socialist agitators (with the exception of the Socialist Reichstag members who were protected by their parliamentary privilege). Bismarck's first anti-Socialist bill was rejected in the Reichstag by an overwhelming majority of 281 to 57, the National Liberals, Catholics, Progressives, and Socialists all voting against it.

Then, after the second attempt on the Emperor, Bismarck at once dissolved the Reichstag, ordered new elections, and called for drastic anti-Socialist legislation. This time he was successful. . . .

Bismarck soon recognized that the anti-Socialist law was not a wholly satisfactory solution of the Socialist menace. The law was merely negative, repressive. Something positive must be done to make the industrial workers better off, and especially to make them feel that the German state was their friend and not their enemy. This was Bismarck's main motive in pushing the social insurance legislation of the early 1880s. This motive is seen in remarks that he let drop and in the provisions that he was very insistent should be included in the insurance laws. He wanted the German state to contribute to the cost of insurance along with employers and employees, so that the worker would feel a sense of gratitude to the state. With less cause for anxiety and with the state as their friend, the workers, Bismarck hoped, would be more contented, and less likely to listen to Socialist agitators. In this way, Bismarck hoped, the power of the Social Democratic Party would be undermined. His hope was not realized and after 1890, during his last years, he seems to have felt that, so far as his political motives were concerned, his social insurance laws were a failure and he showed little pride or interest in them. . . .

An Employer's Liability Act of 1871 was supposed to provide compensation in case a workman was killed or injured by accident. The law, however, was generally recognized to be very inadequate and unsatisfactory. The worker had to prove that the accident was not his own fault, and was consequently often involved in long and costly law suits, and in most cases got no satisfaction at all. During the 1870s Bismarck refused to do anything to improve the law, partly because he was so busy with other matters, partly because he did not want to put upon employers more burdensome cost charges which might weaken their competitive position in foreign markets.

In April 1880, however, a Rhine-Westphalian mining industrialist, Louis Baare, presented a proposal for insuring workers against accident and injury. It met with Bismarck's approval and marks the beginning of his active interest in social insurance and of his pushing of legislation to secure it. He asked Baare to elaborate his proposal into a draft law. At the same time he instructed Theodor Lohmann, one of his own subordinates in the Ministry of Trade, to study Baare's proposal but also to draw up a government draft embodying his own views.

Theodor Lohmann, son of a Westphalian Lutheran pastor, was a deeply religious and conservative man of great ability and staunch independence of character. For years he had devoted much theoretical study and practical investigation to the subject of social welfare. His convictions differed considerably from Bismarck's political calculations. He was opposed to having the state make financial contributions toward paying the insurance premiums because charity weakened the worker's sense of responsibility.

More important in his mind was the fact that if employers and employees by themselves contributed the insurance funds and managed them jointly, then labor and capital would build up a common habit of cooperation and mutual understanding,

and that was the most important thing of all. But Lohmann had
to subordinate his own convictions to Bismarck's wishes, so that
the government draft bill as actually worked out represented
Bismarck's views rather than Lohmann's. . . .

Bismarck's first accident insurance bill, embodying his own
views with suggestions from Baare and Lohmann and drafted
by Lohmann, was laid before the Reichstag in April 1881. Its
novel feature was that it imposed statutory compulsion on many
classes of workers to be insured against accident. All workers
in mining, iron and steel foundries, shipbuilding, and building
construction who received less than 2,000 marks [$500] a year
in wages must be insured. . . .

To emphasize Bismarck's idea of the beneficent part played
by the government the insurance scheme was to be administered
by an Imperial Insurance Bureau which would guarantee the
pension and death payments and thus form a paternal bond between the worker and the government. In the case of poorer
workers (those earning less than 750 marks a year), the state
would also pay one third of the insurance premiums, the other
two thirds being paid by the employers, and the poorer workers
paying nothing. In the case of the better off workers (those
receiving between 750 and 2,000 marks annually), the cost
of the premiums was divided between the employer and the
workers, the state contributing nothing but the cost of administration.

The three main feaures of the bill on which Bismarck
had insisted—compulsion to insure, an Imperial Insurance
Bureau, and state contributions—were precisely the points that
were most attacked and brought the bill to grief.

The National Liberal party, which had been Bismarck's
main support ever since 1866, had split in 1879 when two thirds
of its really liberal members refused to accept Bismarck's protective tariff law and went over to the opposition. They and the
Progressives ably led by Eugen Richter denounced the obligatory
clause as contrary to the liberal principles of laissez faire. They
also criticized the state contribution in the case of poorer workers
as "class legislation" and feared that the money for the state's
contribution would be raised by indirect taxes which bore most

heavily on the classes least able to bear them. (Bismarck in fact always strongly favored indirect rather than direct taxes because the indirect taxes were "concealed" and caused less irritation among people who were not so aware of them as in the case of direct taxes.)

The Catholic Center party, though much divided amongst themselves, were sharply opposed to the Imperial Insurance Bureau as a centralizing encroachment on states rights. As federalists rather than centralists, and having their main strength in Catholic Bavaria, the Catholic Center members were always fearful of Prussia's dominating power in the Empire. Their fears found an echo in many of the smaller German states who likewise opposed a new central insurance bureau.

The Social Democrats condemned all the insurance provisions of the bill because they were put forward by a government to which they were ideologically opposed, and also because of various specific objections.

The bill was disfigured by so many amendments, including one which placed the whole cost on the employers, that Bismarck withdrew the bill and dissolved the Reichstag. A few days before the new Reichstag elections, he made propaganda for a new revised accident insurance bill by having William I issue an Imperial Message on November 17, 1881. It stated that "the cure of social ills must be sought not exclusively in the repression of Social Democratic excesses, but simultaneously in the positive advancement of the welfare of the working classes." It also promised a threefold program of sickness, accident, and old age insurance.

In spite of the Emperor's message, the opposition parties increased their strength in the Reichstag. The second accident insurance bill drafted by Lohmann and laid before the new Reichstag in May 1882 fared no better than the first, because Bismarck would not abandon his idea of a centralized, state-aided, bureaucratic institution. After being criticized and amended, it was eventually replaced by a third accident insurance bill which finally passed the Reichstag in 1884.

Meanwhile Bismarck had better success with sickness insurance. A bill to establish this was quickly passed by the Reichstag and became law on June 15, 1883. It made insurance against sickness obligatory for the great majority of wage earners, but not for the professional classes and other white-collar workers. The law wisely made use of many already existing mutual aid societies, friendly associations, guilds, and local sick benefit funds. Where such sickness funds did not exist, they were created by the law and organized by localities. To pacify Catholics and other states rights critics who dreaded Bismarck's centralizing of state power, the law provided that all the various local sickness funds should be supervised and controlled by the legislatures and insurance bureaus of the different German states instead of being under an Imperial Insurance Bureau.

Contributions were borne jointly, two thirds by the workers and one third by the employers as a rule. In return, the insured received many kinds of benefits in case of sickness:

a. Sickness pay for thirteen weeks (increased in 1903 to twenty-six weeks, and in some cases for a longer period) ;

b. Maternity pay for six weeks after childbirth;

c. Free medical attendance, including free medicines during sickness, and in many cases free maintenance in hospitals, convalescent homes;

d. Generous funeral allowances in case of death.

Each local fund made its own contract with doctors, druggists, and hospitals. Doctors were usually paid either fixed fees for each visit or an over-all lump sum based on the number of the insured. Patients had a free choice of doctors from the panel of practitioners with whom the sickness fund had made contracts.

In 1910 there were over twenty-three thousand statutory sickness funds. Altogether they received 130 million marks from employers and 260 million from workers, and had some small reserves beyond the amounts paid out in sickness benefits. The cost of administration was commendably low—only about 5 per cent of the contributions received.

Bismarck was more a practical opportunist than a man of theories and principles. Having taken note of criticisms and prejudices which his first two accident insurance bills had encountered, he made many revisions and brought in a third accident insurance bill which was easily adopted by the Reichstag in July 1884, and came into operation on October 1, 1885. It introduced compulsory accident insurance on all workers receiving less than 3,000 marks a year and engaged in mining, shipbuilding, factories, and building construction (in 1911 the coverage was extended to include workers in these and almost all other undertakings receiving less than 5,000 marks a year).

The whole cost of insurance was placed upon the employers —no contributions by the worker or by the state. For purposes of administration and management, all employers were organized into mutual associations according to geographical areas and the nature and accidental risk in different undertakings. . . . The main supervisory authority and control continued in the hands of the existing local State Insurance Offices. . . .

The Reich government made the gesture of advancing the money to the post office to pay the accident claims as they were awarded during the year. It was then reimbursed at the end of the year by the employer mutual associations which levied the necessary assessments upon themselves.

Compensation for injury by accident usually (in about 96 per cent of the cases) took the form of a pension, rather than the lump-sum payment usually favored by private insurance companies. This was in accordance with the social idea of providing support to the injured during his disability, or in case of death to his dependent survivors. During the first thirteen weeks, while the case was being investigated and the amount of the pension determined, the injured person received support at once from his sickness fund which was later reimbursed by the mutual association of employers.

The amount of accident pensions for lower income workers was two thirds of the yearly earnings in case of total disability, and proportionately less for partial disability. . . . In the case of higher income workers, where the need was less, the basis of calculation resulted in a pension a little less than two thirds of the yearly earnings. If accident resulted in death, funeral money equal to about a month's earnings was paid, and a pension of one fifth the yearly earnings of the deceased was paid to his widow until her death or remarriage.

Additional payments were made for the benefit of his children and grandchildren and parents and grandparents so far as they had been dependent on him. Pensions were always paid through the post office, usually in advance monthly.

One of the most important indirect results of the accident insurance law was greater care in the prevention of accidents and a sharp decline in their number. The mutual associations were required to issue and enforce regulations for safety and prevention of accidents. These regulations were drawn up after consultation with the workers and then had to be approved by the Imperial Insurance Office. Disregard of them by employer or employees was seriously punished. As an admirable object lesson in accident prevention, there was set up in 1903 in a specially erected building in Charlottenburg, with money granted by the German government, "a permanent exhibition of contrivances for the prevention of accidents." Most of the exhibits were contributed by the various mutual associations and had proved of value in practical use. All out-of-date exhibits were promptly discarded in favor of the most modern improvements.

The third great measure of social insurance—provision for disability and old age—passed the Reichstag and became law on June 22, 1889. It was brought about more by the new, young, self-confident Emperor William II than by the old, disappointed, and disillusioned Iron Chancellor. Bismarck had originally planned to push the measure, in accordance with old Emperor William I's propagandist message of 1881, and would have liked to see the Reich government contribute two thirds of the cost. But he lost interest when the Reichstag made so many criticisms of his accident and sickness proposals and objected so strongly to the idea of large financial contributions by the Reich government. He was also disappointed that his accident and sickness insurance measures seemed to have brought no change of heart on the part of the Social Democrats. They were as hostile and discontented as ever, and their numbers were rapidly mounting at each election. When a great strike of Westphalian coal miners took place in 1888, Bismarck declared that he was ready to use troops to shoot strikers if necessary. William II, on the other hand, did not want to begin his reign with bloodshed. He announced that he would call an international conference to deal with the labor question and ordered that his grandfather's promise of disability and old age insurance should be carried out.

The law of 1889 provided that nearly all wage earners of both sexes over sixteen years of age receiving less than 2,000 marks a year must be insured against disability and old age. The cost was borne equally by employers and employees and by a flat contribution from the Imperial Treasury of 50 marks for each person receiving a disability or old age pension. The system was administered by pension boards organized by the governments of the various German states. Each pension board was made up of elected representatives of employers and employees in equal numbers, presided over by an appointee of the local state government. Disputed matters might be carried to the Imperial Insurance Office created by Bismarck in 1884, but otherwise the principle of states rights was generally observed.

Disability pensions, so far as not covered by sickness or accident benefits, were paid to insured persons who became disabled and who had paid contributions for at least five years. Old age pensions were paid to insured persons, whether able to work or not, who had paid contributions for thirty years and had reached the age of seventy (which cost far less than old age pensions that begin at age sixty-five as is generally the case in the United States). All insured persons were grouped into five classes according to wages received. The joint employer and employee contribution was fixed by the Federal Council on an estimated actuarial basis and varied according to class. The disability and old age pensions varied from 110 marks annually in the lowest class to 230 marks in the first class.

By the end of 1910 nearly two and a half million pensions had been granted and a million were still in force at that date, about 80 per cent on account of disability and 20 per cent on account of old age.

In 1911 all three kinds of social insurance were somewhat expanded (as so often happens) by including some new groups of persons, raising the wage figure below which insurance became compulsory, and by extending the benefits. But the essential features remained unchanged until after World War I.

FIVE WELFARE STATE COUNTRIES [3]

When . . . New Zealand, Australia and the Scandinavian countries "went Labor," the new governments found that many of the industries which British Labor in 1945 undertook to socialize had, in whole or in part, already been brought into the public sector. In some instances these industries had been nationalized as a result of the pressure exerted by the labor and progressive movement while it still occupied the benches of the Opposition; in some instances, as a result of general consumer or public demand.

In New Zealand, for instance, Labor, in 1935, on entering office, took charge of a government which was already operating all railways, telephone, telegraph and radio services and large hydro-electric plants; which controlled seven eighths of the nation's timber and coal reserves; managed life insurance, fire insurance and public trust offices, and conducted health resort services.

In Sweden, the government owned, prior to the formation of the Social Democratic government, the telephone and telegraph systems, the most important railroads, most of the electric power, and over a fifth of the forests. It operated the central bank, the radio system, cigarette manufacture, and the wholesaling of liquor. In addition it held a 50 per cent interest in the capital of the largest iron ore mining company, was a part owner of 85 per cent of all known iron ore resources, and exerted a licensing control over the armament industry.

Banking and Credit: During their term of office the Labor and Social Democratic governments have considerably extended the sphere of public ownership. . . . One of the first major acts of the British Labor government when it assumed office in 1945 was to nationalize the Bank of England. Other Labor and Social Democratic governments have been likewise interested in public control of banking and credit. In New Zealand, the Labor government, soon after its electoral victory of 1935, proceeded

---

[3] From *Labor Governments at Work*, by Harry W. Laidler, executive director, League for Industrial Democracy. The League. New York. '48. p8-17. Reprinted by permission. This section of the pamphlet is devoted to a study of labor government programs in New Zealand, Australia, Sweden, Norway, and Denmark through 1948. It should be read in conjunction with the two following articles, which trace more recent events in New Zealand and Australia.—Editor.

to the enactment of the Reserve Bank Amendment Act of April 1936, providing for the buying out of the private shareholders of the Reserve Bank, the elimination of shareholder directors, and the reconstruction of the institution as "a completely state-owned and state-controlled authority responsible for giving effect to the monetary policy of the government." . . . Under its new powers, the bank made numerous loans to the government to assist in marketing schemes, as well as for general purposes.

The New Zealand Labor government also during its term of office has abolished the semi-private control of the State Advances Corporation, which makes loans to workers for the purchase of their homes; has established state control over the transfer of all funds to and from New Zealand; and has purchased from private owners (in 1945) all of the private share capital in the Bank of New Zealand, the largest trading bank of that country.

Throughout its history, the Australian Labor Party has also shown a keen interest in the public control of many of the banking facilities of the country. In 1912, when Labor was temporarily in office, it created a Commonwealth Bank. For the next twelve years, this bank was operated by a governor but, in 1924, a board representing various groups in the community was substituted for the governor. Labor believed that the policy of the bank's board during the depression of 1929-33 bore harshly on the small businessman and caused much avoidable unemployment and distress. In 1945, to prevent a repetition of an unnecessarily deflationary policy, and to assure the full utilization of the bank as an instrument for full employment, the Labor government passed an act returning the bank's management to the hands of the governor, but giving final say in the determination of public policy to the country's treasurer.

The 1945 act also gave the Commonwealth Bank power to establish bank branches in various parts of the country, and to control in many ways the credit policy of the country. It created an Industrial Finance Department to furnish long-term capital to small industry. It gave the central bank power to determine what general loan policy the country's banks should follow and to provide for control of the credit policy of the country in many other ways.

Other Advances in Public Ownership: The Labor governments during their terms of office have likewise enacted legislation for the enlargement of the nation's control over public utilities, natural resources and other basic industries, as follows:

New Zealand. The government since its inauguration in 1935 has nationalized the internal air services of the Dominion, and has set up a National Airways Corporation to run it; has completed the socialization of the mines and has established an Internal Marketing Division which imports all oranges and bananas needed in the country, and processes and sells to retailers large quantities of butter.

Australia. In 1942, the Australian Labor government, which had taken office the previous year, reorganized the National Broadcasting Services, and provided for a commission of five to take charge of the broadcasts over the Commonwealth-wide network of the national stations, and of the licensing and regulation of the hundred or more commercial stations scattered throughout the country.

In 1945, the Australian government also nationalized its interstate air lines, in keeping with the general Australian policy of keeping transport in public hands. It likewise entered into partnership relations with Great Britain for the operation of the air service between Australia and the United Kingdom and with Great Britain and New Zealand for the operation of the British Commonwealth Pacific Airlines. The Australian Labor government, since the war, has also initiated a long-range program for the reconstruction of the nation's railroads, including the adoption of uniform gauges for state and federal railways.

Sweden. In 1935 . . . the state purchased a majority of stocks of the Air Transport Company, which it had previously subsidized, appointed government directors and brought the airways into active cooperation with the railway administration. In 1938, it transferred to the state the rights of the landowners to ores that may be found in the future on private property. . . .

Norway. Since World War II, the Norwegian Labor government has assumed control of numerous basic industries. In 1946, after the war, the government undertook the construction of a super-modern electro-iron works located in Mo i Rana, in northern Norway—one of the largest single industrial ventures in the history of the country. In the corporation controlling this enterprise, the government holds a majority of stocks. In 1947, the government also bought the iron ore deposits of the Dunderland Iron Ore Company with an estimated output of from one half to one million metric tons.

The Labor-controlled Norwegian Storting also decided in the years following the occupation to form a big industrial company to take over and complete some of the huge industries planned by the Germans during their occupation for the long-term development of the country. The new Norwegian state-owned company immediately set to work to complete a large aluminum plant at Aardal, and to take over power plants.

The postwar period also found the Norwegian government in possession of a majority of shares of the Norsk Hydro, one of Norway's largest electro-chemical firms which controlled hydro-electric generating plants and important aluminum works. The majority of stocks of this firm was held before the war by French interests.

The Labor government since the war has likewise initiated state monopolies in the importation of grains, solid fuels and medical supplies and the construction and operation of quick-freeze plants in northern Norway. It has undertaken the operation of a nation-wide chain of agricultural machinery stations; has initiated a fifteen-year reconstruction and electrification plan for the state-owned railways and a broad general plan of electrification, and is cooperating with other Scandinavian countries in the formation of a Scandinavian air service between Norway and North and South America.

Housing: All of the Labor governments, as might be expected, have given much attention since their inception to the housing of their people and have initiated many public and co-operative housing ventures. The New Zealand Labor government, following its election to office in 1935, felt, in the words of Deputy Prime Minister Nash, that it had the duty "to carry good shelter as well as good food, good clothing, good education, good health and working conditions to the people, not to some of the people only, but to all the people all the time."

One of its earliest activities in the field of housing was the mobilization of its resources for the construction of thousands of modern individual houses in more than a hundred and fifty cities and towns. Those homes were made available to all classes of the community without discrimination and no income bar or means test was employed in the selection of tenants. The homes built under this program showed an attractiveness and pleasing variety which private builders had failed to achieve. . . .

The Commonwealth of Australia, in June 1946, set itself the goal of fifty thousand new houses a year to be erected by public and private agencies. Under the arrangement agreed upon, the federal government helps with the financing, while the Australian states build and rent the houses to the tenants. As in several other countries, the rents charged are geared to the occupants' incomes, and families earning the basic wage are not required to pay more than one fifth of their incomes for rent, regardless of the economic rent of their apartments. The Commonwealth Bank also makes loans at lowest practicable interest rates to building societies and to those wishing to own their own homes, while each state provides homes for sale to persons of limited incomes on little or no advance deposit.

The Scandinavian countries under Labor and Social Democratic control have also been famous for the housing programs of their governments, as well as of their cooperative societies. In numerous instances, the governments have supplied funds and technical advice and supervision to cooperative societies, while the cooperative building societies have taken charge of the administration of the housing ventures. In most cities of Scandinavia, as a result of these undertakings, slums, to all intents and purposes, have disappeared.

In Norway, outside of the extensive housing program initiated by the government in Oslo and other cities in central and southern Norway, the government has recently undertaken a comprehensive building program in the sixty thousand square miles of the devastated Finnmark and Norland area in North Norway. In these districts whole towns are being planned and constructed.

In Denmark, following the inauguration of the Social Democratic government in 1947, a special Ministry of Building was established to further the construction of homes for the Danish people.

Social Insurance: The Australasian and Scandinavian labor governments have also been pioneers in the field of social insurance. The British Commonwealth Dominion of New Zealand, in fact, initiated in 1938 a social insurance system which gave the most complete coverage of any social insurance plans passed by any legislature in the world up to that time, and which became, in many ways, a model for the British social insurance act of a decade later. Today the government, through its social security system, protects the individual against financial loss occasioned by sickness, invalidity, old age, unemployment, orphanhood and occupational disease. Its old age pension system reaches down to those [arriving] at the age of sixty. Its unemployment insurance benefits are paid as long as a person is unemployed, unless, of course, he has become eligible to receive another class of benefit. As a means of protecting the child, the government gives, upon application, ten shillings a week for the maintenance of any child under sixteen.

Besides this, the Labor government makes available free health and hospital services to every citizen irrespective of income. As in the case of the British national health service, the citizen in need may select his own physician, the doctor selected collecting his fee either from the government or from the patient. If the patient pays, he recovers from the state. A physician living in a sparsely settled district may arrange to treat all patients in the district. In such a case, the government pays the physician a stated salary.

All medicines prescribed by the physician under the plan are free. If a patient goes to a private hospital, the government makes a grant to the hospital equivalent to the cost of treatment in a public hospital. In maternity cases, benefits continue fourteen days after childbirth. Since World War II, dental treatment has been extended to all persons up to nineteen years of age. As for the financing of the system, this is accomplished by payments by both the state and employees. A social security tax of about 7.5 per cent at present writing is being levied on wages, salaries and company earnings. Social security benefits from 1935 to 1945 increased about eleven fold.

In Australia, the country was handicapped for years in providing a comprehensive social insurance system as a result of the Australian legal setup which left to individual states in the Commonwealth all social insurance legislation except that dealing with old age pensions and invalidity protection. In late 1946, however, the Labor government submitted a referendum authorizing the Commonwealth to make laws with respect to all forms of social legislation. This was carried by a comfortable majority, and the Constitution was amended as from December 19, 1946, so as to empower the Commonwealth Parliament, in addition to the invalid and old age pensions power, to make laws with respect to "the provision of maternity allowances, widow pensions, child endowments, unemployment, pharmaceutical, sickness and hospital benefits, medical and dental services, benefits to students and family allowances." Since this amendment went into effect, the government has been at work bringing the social insurance system more in line with that in New Zealand and Great Britain. . . .

In Scandinavia, the social insurance system up until World War II was conducted largely in conjunction with trade unions, the governments granting subsidies to the insurance funds. In January 1946, however, the Riksdag passed legislation providing for obligatory health insurance and increased old age pensions, the health insurance provisions to go into effect by July 1, 1950. . . . Included in the postwar social legislation have been free vacation travel for children of parents and for mothers of families in lower income groups, and free school lunches for all.

Among the postwar developments in Norway in the field of social insurance have been legislation for children's allowances, a broadened health insurance program, and a national dental insurance scheme. Funds earmarked for social affairs in the Norwegian budget have steadily increased here as well as in the little progressive Scandinavian country of Denmark.

Planning for Full Employment: One of the most insistent demands of democratic Socialists has been that for elimination of mass unemployment. Most Socialists believe that depressions, with their accompanying armies of the unemployed, cannot be eliminated under a system of capitalism with its lack of social planning and its monopolistic trends. Economic security with freedom, they contend, can only be attained under a democratically planned Socialist system.

They feel, however, that much can be done under the capitalist order to stabilize industry and to alleviate, if not cure, the evil of mass unemployment. This is particularly true when, as in the Scandinavian countries, there are large trade union and cooperative movements bent on keeping consumer purchasing power on a high level; when public utilities and certain other important services are under public ownership and management, and when the government has control of key banking and credit agencies.

The Social Democratic government of Sweden and the Labor government of New Zealand attained office in their respective countries during the days of the depression of the 1930s. Both of these governments gave much attention to measures for grappling with the economic crisis. After the election of 1932 and before Parliament assembled, a commission was appointed by the Swedish government to survey work schemes which public and semi-public bodies could put into immediate execution. The report, submitted December 3, 1932, listed thirty-two hundred individual undertakings that could be started within a short time, with detailed information regarding their nature and the expenses involved. It likewise noted others about which more information regarding needed outlay had to be gathered.

The first plan for meeting the crisis in Sweden was approved by Parliament in June 1933, and from then to the end of 1936, approximately $100 million was spent on public works projects designed to give employment to the jobless. The effect of this program "spread to all corners of Sweden. Something like a hundred thousand minor and major undertakings, public, semi-public and private, benefited. Public buildings, hospitals, schools, dwellings, roads, bridges, harbors, watering and drainage systems, power stations, and playing fields are among the lasting monuments," as Dr. Braatoy declares, "to the crisis policy of Sweden's Social Democratic governments."

During this period, most of the workers were taken out of the category of relief workers, and were employed under conditions prevailing in the general labor market, constituting a revolution in the method of caring for the unemployed. The last several million dollars for public works for the jobless was allocated in 1937. By July 1937, when there were still many millions unemployed in the United States, the registered jobless in Sweden had shrunk to 9,800, chiefly in the forestry and quarrying districts, and, by mid-1938, jobless in these areas had been reduced by over nine tenths from the 1933 figures.

Besides initiating the construction of public works, the Swedish Social Democratic government during the 1930s utilized its state-owned banking and credit facilities to expand and contract credit, to prevent undue fluctuations in foreign exchanges, to provide additional credit to smaller undertakings that had difficulty in financing economically sound expansion, and to enlarge its control over loans to industrial enterprises.

The Social Democratic government likewise subsidized and guaranteed the production of numerous food products; encouraged the growth of the cooperative movement; made extensive grants for the rehousing of the people and the improvement of living quarters of farm hands; raised old age pension rates; expanded health facilities; reduced the maximum working week in agriculture and among Swedish seamen; and improved its taxation system.

The New Zealand Labor government, when it went into office in 1935, likewise set itself the task of giving work to its army of unemployed, the numbers of which had risen during the early thirties to unprecedented heights. Through measures somewhat similar to those adopted in Sweden—the use of banking and credit facilities, housing, national development works, restoration of cuts in wages, pensions and social services, establishment of a forty-hour week, etc.—the government brought at least temporary stability to New Zealand industry and reduced unemployment to a minimum.

Following the war, the Labor Party approved a comprehensive five-year plan in behalf of a rising standard of living and greater economic security. Rejecting the idea that "the country's affairs should be left to the play of the blind forces of selfish and unplanned private interests," it pledged itself to legislation for the expansion of its programs in the fields of housing, education, public works, agriculture, industry, research, land conservation, transportation and communication, labor and social insurance legislation. It outlined the most extensive plan for the development of New Zealand's natural resources in the country's history. The party also gave much attention to ways and means of guaranteeing recreational opportunities to all in future years when technological developments should bring greater leisure to the country's workmen.

In Australia the Labor government also, since its inauguration in 1941, has given much thought to measures for averting mass unemployment. In 1945, it issued a White Paper on Full Employment, in which it pledged itself to pursue a policy in behalf of jobs for all, to be carried out "with the utmost energy and determination." In Norway and Denmark similar programs have been initiated. In Norway Production Councils, an Economic Coordination Council, and a Money and Finance Council were established after the war to assist in preventing the continuance of the old cycle of boom and bust. . . .

While Labor and Social Democratic governments cannot be credited with all the recent social gains in Australasia and the Scandinavian countries, any more than they can be denounced for the injury to the countries' economies wrought by war and its aftermath, they can be rightly acclaimed for many of the remarkable advances which the common people have made since Labor's advent to power.

SOCIALISTS LOSE IN NEW ZEALAND [4]

Voters in New Zealand are somewhat surprised to see how seriously the rest of the world is taking their decision to throw

⁴ From "Socialists Lose, Socialism Stays." Reprinted from U.S. News & World Report, an independent weekly magazine on national and international affairs, published at Washington, D.C. Copyright 1950, United States News Publishing Company. 27:24-5. December 9, 1949.

out the Labor party that has ruled the country for fourteen years.

As New Zealanders see it, they just voted for a change. They did not vote for an end to the welfare state. Since 1898, long before Socialists took over, New Zealand has been out in front of the rest of the world with old-age pensions and welfare benefits.

The Nationalist party now coming to power [as a result of the parliamentary election in November 1949] does not propose to change or to interfere with social welfare programs. But the newcomers do promise to reduce some of the government controls and to cut some of the taxes now soaking up almost a third of national income.

For politicians in the United States and Britain, the upset of the Labor party Socialists should show simply that formulas for getting votes, promises of more and more of the same, do not last forever. The public decides that it should try some other leaders and see whether they can do as well or better.

What happened in New Zealand isn't necessarily a sign of what will happen in the United States or in Britain. In the United States it has been seventeen years since there was a vote for a change at the top. In Britain, the Labor government has been in power since 1945. . . . People in both countries can learn much from what happened in New Zealand, but only if there is an understanding of the country and its problems. . . .

Issues before the voters were relatively few. Labor stood on a record that even the Nationalists admitted was a good one. The Nationalists said, in effect, that they wouldn't change much, but that they would manage things better.

Government in business, thus, wasn't really an issue. In housing, for example, the Labor government in ten years has built twenty thousand new homes at a cost of $100 million. These houses, modern in design, compare favorably with the best United States low-income housing save that they lack central heating, which is not popular in New Zealand's mild climate. The Nationalist government will continue building homes and operating nationalized banks, railroads, radio broadcasting, the telegraph system, coal mines and other industries.

Social security was not an issue either. About one third of the government's budget goes to social security, but the Nationalists promise to spend no less. New Zealand, they say, can afford it.

Old age pensions, for example, take 7.5 per cent of the gross income of all workers and 7.5 per cent of the net income of all employers. For this, a worker can get up to one third of his annual income per year when he retires at sixty-five. Any New Zealander, irrespective of income, is eligible for a pension. The plan is not self-supporting; the government makes up the deficit.

Free medicine in New Zealand is not quite as complete as the British Labor government's plan and it operates differently. In New Zealand, the patient pays his own doctor bill and gets a refund from the government. In Britain, the government pays the physicians.

State controls and prices were major issues. The Nationalists promised to cut both controls and prices.

Government control of foodstuffs, however, is tied up with New Zealand's almost unanimous desire to help Britain through the mother country's current economic crisis. Housewives in New Zealand, for example, still market under a wartime zoning system that requires them to buy such things as butter, cheese, eggs and fruit at certain stores. Aim is to keep down consumption in order to send more to Britain. But New Zealanders are tired of filling out forms and of going to government offices for all sorts of things. They want fewer controls. Rising prices have irritated New Zealanders. . . .

Just how the Nationalists will go about reducing controls and prices remains to be seen. As a starter, the new government may cut the number of people on its pay roll, currently about one fifth of the working population. Jobs are easy to find, however. Only a hundred and fifty people in the country are listed as unemployed and job vacancies total more than twenty-five thousand.

SOCIALISTS LOSE IN AUSTRALIA [5]

Until December 10 [1949] Australia was ruled, as most democratic countries have been since World War II, by a labor-oriented government. Now this country is to have a government whose closest ties are with business and agriculture. For the West, this is an important test case.

A preview at least of Australia's answer to this question can be given now, on the basis of the election campaign waged by the victorious Liberal-Country party. In outline here's what the new government plans to do:

Call a halt to Labor's nationalization program—and rescind some of the nationalization legislation already adopted.

Ease up on government controls of business, stopping the trend toward a managed economy.

Crack down on the power of labor union leaders.

Keep Labor's public welfare program virtually intact, perhaps even extend it.

Thus, Australian businessmen expect a better break from the [Robert] Menzies government than they have been getting for the past eight years under Labor. But they don't imagine for a minute that Australia is to have a free-wheeling economy from which all traces of socialism will be removed.

True, Menzies seems to have won the election by his attacks on nationalization and the managed economy. He made real capital out of Labor's attempt two years ago to nationalize commercial banking. For even though this venture in socialism already had been stymied by the courts, Labor still had banking in its nationalization program, along with insurance, shipping, public health, radio services, and sugar refining.

However, when it came to the welfare side of socialism, Menzies took a me-too line—and probably would have lost the election if he hadn't.

Maintaining the social services will mean a heavy government spending program. And Menzies is also committed to expanded defense expenditures. So Australian businessmen see

[5] From "When Socialism Is Defeated." *Business Week*. p53-4. December 24, 1949. Reprinted by permission.

little hope of any relief in the tax policies of the new government. . . .

The Menzies program for reversing the Socialist trend in Australia is this:

The bank nationalization act will be repealed, and a constitutional amendment will make it impossible for such Socialist legislation to be passed in future without a popular referendum.

The government airlines set up by Labor will be sold out to private operators—unless they can pay their own way. Labor legislation setting up state monopolies in radio and television will probably be rescinded. The same goes for the planned federal operation of coastal shipping.

Banking and credit controls will be retained. But now they will be handled by the independent board which is supposed to supervise the operations of the country's central bank. Under the Labor government this board had been replaced by a single governor who took his orders from the federal treasury.

Militant labor union tactics are to be curbed by compulsory secret ballots in all elections of union officials and in all strike decisions. The Communist party is to be outlawed.

Menzies has also promised to cut down Australia's top heavy bureaucracy. But some controls are sure to stay, including those on bank credit policy and new capital issues, raw material allocation, import and export licenses. Even in business circles some of these are considered essential as long as the demand for scarce resources remains strong.

Nor does Menzies have any intention of interfering with the economic activities of the state governments. Railroads have been state monopolies from the beginning. Most of Australia's electric power is controlled by state or municipal authorities. And some state governments have gone into road transport and other fields of industry.

The Federal Government itself is now building an aluminum plant. Also it owns stock in an oil refinery, in a bus-building plant, in radio manufacturing, and in a telegraph company. These interests will be kept for the time being, at least.

The fact is that paternalistic government has been characteristic of Australia since the nineteenth century. This is partly because Australia was originally a British penal colony; for a long period the government's chief role was as a warden of convicts.

When it comes to welfare economics, Menzies' position shapes up about this way:

He favors a national health scheme which involves government subsidies to hospitals. He has promised full support of the present systems of national insurance against sickness, old age, widowhood, and unemployment. The big change likely in the medical field: reversal of Labor's plan for free medicines.

The chances are that before the next election Menzies will try to extend the whole insurance setup—though on a contributory basis. Menzies even outbid Labor on the "baby bonus" question. Up to now, every child after the first has been subsidized. Menzies has promised a bonus for the first as well.

The new government also favors a system of farm price supports that doesn't differ much from the Brannan Plan in the United States. And Menzies wants the government to take a more aggressive lead in developing the new resources in the interior of Australia.

WAYS AHEAD—A VARIETY OF VIEWS

EDITOR'S INTRODUCTION

The five selections which follow do not necessarily argue for or against the welfare state as we have discussed it, but each is tangentially related to the problem.

1. The President's message to Congress on a new welfare department for his cabinet sets forth the machinery through which Mr. Truman would like to carry out many Fair Deal welfare proposals. Under the Reorganization Act of 1949, such presidential reorganization steps take effect sixty days after being presented to Congress, unless either House or Senate votes them down. On July 10, 1949, the House did just this, voting to disapprove the proposal 249-71, and thus killing the measure at least for the sessions of the 81st Congress. This was the second rebuff the President had received on the welfare department proposal. The Senate had rejected a similar measure in 1949.

2. Norman Thomas, veteran leader of the Socialist party of the United States, has a special reason for concern with the welfare state controversy. Many welfare state opponents argue that the present national administration is leading us to socialism, or has, indeed, already brought us to a socialistic state. Defendants of welfare state measures deny this, with equal emphasis. And, in the midst of it all, the actual doctrinaire view of the Socialists (openly avowing allegiance to socialism) is usually lost. Mr. Thomas presents his views on the welfare state which, he maintains, does not mix with the free enterprise system.

3. Henry A. Wallace, member of the New Deal inner sanctum in the 1930s and early 1940s, presents still another view. Totally at odds with the Truman Administration (at least until his resignation from the Progressive party in August 1950), he

supports the welfare state through what he calls "planned abundance." He recalls with irony the furor raised years ago about his "ever normal granary" plan—a furor which seems mild indeed, in comparison with today's discussion of the Brannan Plan, health insurance and other proposed Fair Deal measures.

4. David E. Lilienthal, once more a private citizen, speaks with the experience of having pioneered two tremendous government undertakings—the Tennessee Valley Authority and the United States Atomic Energy Commission. His plea for decentralization does not discuss welfare state measures in particular. He is concerned, in this selection from his new book, with methods rather than measures. In effect, he offers to both critics and supporters of the welfare state a way to live with ever-growing governmental functions. He sets forth an objective which might easily be welcomed by all sides—greater "citizen participation" to nourish the strength of our democracy.

5. Finally, Sir Alexander Gray presents a wise and witty challenge—again directed to both opponents and proponents of the welfare state. In a subtle, penetrating way, Sir Alexander presents alternative roads ahead. Whether or not the reader accepts these as the only "preliminary conditions" is not the main point. Speaking with detached wisdom, Sir Alexander presents a point of view which raises the hurly-burly and heat of the welfare state controversy to the level of philosophy.

DEPARTMENT OF HEALTH, EDUCATION, AND SECURITY [1]

To the Congress of the United States: I transmit herewith Reorganization Plan No. 27 of 1950, prepared in accordance with the provisions of the Reorganization Act of 1949. This plan will create a Department of Health, Education and Security, as one of the Executive Departments of the government, and will transfer to it the functions and constituent units of the Federal Security Agency. The Department will be headed by

[1] From a message to Congress from President Harry S. Truman. Released to the press May 31, 1950.

a Secretary of Health, Education and Security, who will be vested with essentially the same duties and authority as are now vested in the Federal Security Administrator.

It is unnecessary to recite again the considerations which make the creation of such a department desirable. As I pointed out in my message transmitting Reorganization Plan No. 1 of 1949, such action has repeatedly been recommended by my predecessors and myself, as well as by others who have studied our government organization. The scope and importance of the functions of the Federal Security Agency plainly warrant departmental status. I feel that there should be no further delay in effecting this essential reorganization.

The present plan is designed to meet the major objections which were raised in opposition to the 1949 plan when it was disapproved by the Senate [on August 16, 1949]. A principal criticism of the 1949 plan was that, in centralizing all statutory authority in the Secretary, as recommended by the Commission on Organization of the Executive Branch of the Government, the plan threatened in matters of health and education unduly to subordinate professional judgment to nonprofessional domination. The present plan is not open to this criticism.

Under the present plan, the Surgeon General and the Commissioner of Education retain all the statutory authority and duties now vested in them. The Public Health Service and the Office of Education remain intact as statutory entities with statutory functions. The Surgeon General and the Commissioner of Education will have the same relationship to the Secretary of the new department that they now have to the Federal Security Administrator.

Furthermore, the present plan provides that the Surgeon General and the Commissioner of Education, along with the Commissioner of Social Security, will report directly to the Secretary. This provision assures that these officials can deal directly with the Secretary in the performance of all matters in their respective fields of responsibility, and the Secretary will thus be in a position to transmit their views to the President and the Congress. It represents an additional safeguard against the fear of the possibility that the views of these officials could be unduly subordinated.

A further difference between this plan and last year's plan is in the name of the new department. In the minds of some the title "Department of Welfare," which was used in the 1949 plan, did not adequately comprehend the health and educational functions and implied their subordination. To avoid any possible misunderstanding, the present plan uses the longer and more explicit title, "Department of Health, Education and Security." . . .

To the extent that this plan would give departmental status to the agency administering the social security and education functions, it is in accord with the one recommendation of the Commission on Organization of the Executive Branch for the creation of a new executive department. I recognize, as I did last year, that the Commission made a further recommendation with respect to the organization of the health functions of the government. The adoption of this plan will not in any way interfere with further adjustments in the functions of the new department either by statute or reorganization plan. . . .

The reorganization plan will go far toward providing the status and type of organization which the magnitude and importance of the functions now administered by the Federal Security Agency demand. It will facilitate coordination with other major segments of the executive branch through the granting of Cabinet status. It will provide a more adequate supervisory structure and will contribute to administrative efficiency and economy. Consistent with the reorganization act itself, the plan neither provides for any new program nor extends or enlarges existing programs beyond the scope of present legislation.

While it is not practicable at this time to estimate the savings that will accrue from the plan, modest but worthwhile economies will result from the factors already cited together with the authority conferred by the plan to improve the administration of the services common to the various agencies of the department.

The creation of this new department is long overdue. While I do not believe that the criticisms advanced against Plan No. 1 of 1949 were well founded, the present plan has been substantially modified to meet them. I recognize that as a result the present plan falls short of what I would regard, and what the Commission on Organization regarded, as the clearest lines of responsibility and authority within executive departments. Nevertheless, in my judgment, the present plan is still an important step forward toward better organization of the executive branch. It provides an adequate basis for establishing this new executive department. I strongly urge that the Congress allow this reorganization plan to become effective.

WELFARE STATE AND FREE ENTERPRISE DON'T MIX [2]

I am . . . committed to the proposition that America, with her resources and technology, can abolish poverty. One element in any program to that end must be a recognition that children born into our national family are entitled to minimum guarantees for health, education, employment and an honorable old age.

Nevertheless, I am far from happy about our present progress toward social security under what is now often called—and curiously, as if it were a term of obloquy—"the welfare state." Let me list in order my reasons for concern:

1. A welfare program is pushed on a hit-or-miss basis without coordination. Each special group tries to grab for itself and compromises are arrived at by a process of logrolling rather than rationality.

2. There is too much of a tendency to consider government a kind of Santa Claus, a failure to recognize that a high level of welfare is possible only if we individually have a high sense of responsibility for the whole process of production and distribution. In time, a program of keeping the Roman proletariat quiet

    [2] From "Democratic Welfare Program Possible Only Under Democratic Socialism," by Norman Thomas, Socialist party leader. *Labor and Nation*. 6:18-19. Winter 1949-50. Reprinted by permission.

by bread and circuses did contribute to the downfall of a great empire. Any modern equivalent of such a program may have a similar result unless there is a conscious development among the people of democratic responsibility for the productive process, for the quality of government agencies, and the general rationality of a social security program.

3. Specifically, a balanced program of social security which can be called genuinely democratic requires immense improvements in government machinery and techniques. I believe in reasonable decentralization but unfortunately few if any of our states are natural economic units. States rights tend to be workers' wrongs. Differences between levels of old age assistance, workmen's compensation and unemployment insurance, etc., in the same general economic areas lead to great friction. Many states are quite unable adequately to support education, to say nothing of additional services. Hence the whole problem of the relation of the federal and state governments must be thought through at all levels. Government machinery must be made more efficient. Bureaucracy—in its bad sense—must be curbed and ways found, while protecting government workers against injustice, to reward excellence and weed out incompetence.

4. More attention must be given to choosing for high office men not only of ability but of honor, transcending a mere success in keeping out of jail. The ease with which liberals and labor leaders endorse good fellows who will shout the right slogans, regardless of their personal standards of honor and responsibility in the performance of duty, is disquieting.

5. It will be extraordinarily difficult if not impossible to deal with the points I have been making as long as we persist in the nonsense that the basic principle of our social and economic conduct is free enterprise. Logically, that term made a little sense in laissez faire days. Those days are gone forever. Yet we are confronted with the phenomenon that most of our active advocates of this or that type of welfare legislation and government control feel obliged to give lip service to private capitalism and the compatibility of the general welfare with the supremacy of the profit motive.

This line of reasoning deprives welfare legislation of a philosophical basis except as a competitive grab game for different groups. If the outstanding principle of evolution and the law of social progress is the survival of the fittest in a capitalist scramble, then it is hard to justify welfare legislation or efficiently to supervise it under democratic control. We are on much sounder ground when we accept Peter Kropotkin's well established theory of mutual aid as a factor in evolution and recognize that our modern technology requires that our supreme loyalty must be to the principle of cooperation.

In the service of that principle we may use a powerful state but we must be zealous to preserve in it a respect for individual rights and individual liberties. Conceivably we might have a welfare state conducted on the principle, "milk from contented cows."

It will be obvious . . . that I have been arguing that a really sound and democratic welfare program requires democratic socialism. . . . I must . . . insist that the motivations of life are too important and its complexities too great to believe that we can arrive at the good society simply by a series of uncorrelated measures pushed through by pressure groups. We need the kind of philosophy and program that democratic socialism provides.

"PLANNING FOR ABUNDANCE" REQUIRED [3]

The outstanding characteristic of the world during the past hundred and fifty years has been the definite but unequal development of different areas toward putting into effect the "general welfare state." Mankind has been slowly and painfully evolving during the past five hundred years away from the state of feudalism toward the general welfare state. In England, the United States, and western Europe the first step after the abandonment of the age of status was into the age of contract or

[3] From an address by Henry A. Wallace, former United States Vice President and 1948 Progressive Party candidate for President, delivered before Progressive Party's National Conference on Jobs and the Economic Crisis, Cleveland, Ohio, September 17, 1949. Printed by permission.

free initiative. People suddenly found themselves no longer
tied to a particular job or a particular piece of land. They
could shop around. Businessmen suddenly found they could do
business without depending on the crown of some great noble,
or the Church. The creative energies unleashed by the end of
feudalism and the advent of free enterprise gave almost complete dominance in world affairs for a hundred and fifty years
to western Europe, England, and the United States. Unfortunately Germany and Japan emerged from feudalism only
two or three generations ago, Russia only a generation ago,
and most of eastern Asia has not yet come out of the chrysalis
of ancient feudalistic disciplines.

It is inevitable that the free enterprise state based on the
Manchester school of economics, in its ruthless competition for
power and profit should forget human rights and develop ever
greater swings in the business cycle of boom and bust. . . . The
anarchy of the free enterprise state is bound to come to an end
from its own instability. The chief question has been whether
the emerging general welfare state should be based on democratic
or totalitarian principles. . . .

The general welfare state which must be born if humanity
is to be saved absolutely requires planning for abundance by
the best brains in the United States. When I say planning for
the welfare state, I am not talking about planned economy in a
Marxist sense, but I am talking about planning in all those key
areas which are absolutely essential if the great depression is
either to be prevented or cured. I am talking about the planning
for the development of our natural resources and the planning
for the expansion of our factories and mills and those fundamental industries which are basic if we are to have twice as
much production in 1970 as we have today. The general welfare state does not require government ownership of all the
means of production as the Marxists envision—but it may require government guidance of many key industries unless the
men directing the great corporations suddenly become convinced
of the absolute necessity of the welfare state in order, in the

long run, to save their own corporate lives and their ability to serve the people as the people should be served.

The general welfare state is of necessity an abundance state —a state in which the government may have to step in and regulate prices, just as it regulates interest rates today. What is sound business sense for the small businessman is not sound business sense for the large businessman in the general welfare state. Jesus stated a fundamental truth for great corporations when he said, "He that loseth his life shall save it." This approach to economic problems has long characterized central banking as distinguished from local banking. When the central bankers in time of crisis and rapidly developing depression raise interest rates, call loans, sell securities and refuse to make new loans they produce an intensification of the very situation which they are preparing to meet. I cannot criticize the small man for acting prudently in terms of his limited experience but the large man must either show statesmanship and ability to plan in terms of the general welfare or the government itself must step in and end unemployment.

The great corporations do not show statesmanship when they refuse wage increases or keep prices high or their profits rising at a time when the great need is to increase the purchasing power of the mass of people, give them more of the goods of life, and distribute a more equal share of the national income. Nor does the administration show statesmanship when it embarks on policies that only accentuate the gap between profits and wages, between sellers and buyers of homes and goods, between industrial prices and farm prices. Planning for the general welfare would have resulted in a far different [1949] Steel Fact Finding Report—and a far different rent and housing program— and a really effective farm program to bring more food to consumers and more income to farmers.

In the agricultural field I personally have had quite a bit to do with planning for abundance to protect the consumer while at the same time the income of the farmers was increased. While the present administration doesn't seem to care to use the phrase "Ever Normal Granary," I know that this concept of the ever normal granary as a protection for both farmer and consumer will not die. It is one of the outstanding examples of planning in the welfare state and when hooked up with soil conservation, especially in the years when the granary is overflowing, it becomes a mechanism for continuing prosperity instead of the alternating boom and bust based on variations in the weather. Sir John Orr, the grand old liberal of England, wanted—when he was in the FAO [United Nations Food and Agriculture Organization]—to expand this concept on a world-wide scale. In so trying he was fought by the Tories of England and the bankers of Wall Street who had their influence through the State Department.

Yes, we must have real planning on a world-wide scale if a democratic general welfare state is to be safe anywhere in the world. The American Tories will call this globaloney and quarts of milk for the Hottentots on the Danube. I say it is commonsense and that in the long run capitalism will never survive in western Europe and the United States unless some such program as this is followed. By one route or another the general welfare will be served. The nations which have emerged most recently from feudalism will be more impatient about the service of the general welfare than we in the United States and Britain who have had a hundred and fifty years of free enterprise experience in a situation where we had vast natural resources and hundreds of millions of people to exploit.

DECENTRALIZATION—ANSWER TO BIG
GOVERNMENT [4]

Democracy, to be truly responsive to our aspirations for individual freedom, must increasingly develop and nourish and strengthen local institutions of government. Few precepts of American life are more deeply felt than this.

In actual practice, however, this policy has given way to a tendency that is its very opposite; an unbroken, and to me dis-

[4] From *This I Do Believe*, by David E. Lilienthal, former chairman, United States Atomic Energy Commission. Harper & Brothers. New York. 1949. p73-83, 88-91. Copyright, 1949, by David E. Lilienthal. Reprinted by permission.

quieting, increase in centralization of administration in Washington.

Here is a direct contradiction between the way we want our institutions of government to function, and the way in fact they do function. Some of those who bear responsibility for this weakening of democracy are unaware of the effect of what they are doing. Others, however, defenders or apologists for the trend, assert that centralized control by Congress and by the administrators in Washington cannot be avoided. Some public administrators and experts in government appear to be now in the process of seeking to persuade the American people that Big Government is inevitable.

I deny that Big Government is inevitable. I assert that there is a workable alternative, and that we should pursue that alternative to ever bigger Big Government. There is no wave of the future before which the American people and their great heritage of localized democracy are powerless.

To judge by what people say on this subject there is hardly anyone in private or public life who is in favor of what is taking place. And yet it goes right on, and at an accelerated pace. Surely this is a curious situation. Some of the most outspoken opponents of centralization I know (judging by their speeches) propose or support legislative controls or appropriation "riders" that make Washington control ever tighter. As a consequence one more prospect for genuine decentralization of federal administration is dimmed or killed. By the same act they turn their back on still another opportunity to delegate to local, state, or federal regional agencies functions that need not be and should not be administered by Washington bureaus nor controlled by the federal Congress.

Federal aid to education provides an important illustration. There is almost universal *verbal* assent to the proposition that federal financial support to education should avoid any trace of control from the Congress and the federal departments in Washington.

But what has actually happened? The evidence is unmistakable that during the past twenty years (with support from both political parties), the trend has been in the other direction, and continues in that direction today.

The land grant college system, with its origin back in Lincoln's administration, provided the country a tested pattern whereby local and state institutions concerned with education could appropriately and productively receive federal funds without the Congress and the Washington executive agencies sticking their fingers into education. Under one guise or another, however, the land grant college principle and practice has been steadily weakened. An opportunity for further decentralization in education has been lost. The new policy of federal financial aid to the school systems of the states makes this recent history all the more a matter of practical and immediate concern.

Atomic energy development provides another illustration. The Atomic Energy Act of 1946 continued the Federal Government as the proprietor of the most extensive scientific, educational, and industrial enterprise in all history. There is no alternative to federal ownership, under present world conditions. . . . The Atomic Energy Commission recognized the dangers of excessive centralization in the Commission and remote control from Washington inherent in this nationalized enterprise, born of war. Since it was not possible nor desirable for the national government to divest itself of the ownership and over-all responsibility for the huge plants, laboratories, uranium refining operations, and research projects, a measure of decentralized administration appeared to the Commission as the best alternative that was open. That was the course followed. Extensive delegations, under broad contracts, were made from this federal Commission to all manner of non-federal institutions, including institutions of higher learning. . . .

In a further effort to avoid excessive Washington office control the Commission set up regional operating offices throughout the country, in charge of Managers of Operations. The managers are given broad authority and responsibility; they are not mere chief clerks, or paper shufflers, who must telephone Washington before making any decisions. (It is not well understood that decentralization is by no means synonymous with moving federal officials out of Washington, into regional offices. If those field officials do not have a large measure of authority to make decisions, this is not decentralization at all, but only a rather expensive form of centralization.)

Such steps taken by the Atomic Energy Commission constitute a first step in the direction of avoiding the bane of Washington overcentralization. . . .

The general trend toward centralization and Washington control, however, makes the Commission's effort to avoid the worst evils of Big Government in atomic energy quite difficult to sustain. Sentiment in Congress for tighter and tighter controls from Washington to be exercised by the Commission or congressional committees or the Bureau of the Budget tend to cancel efforts to encourage greater responsibility and initiative in the field, beyond the Washington scene.

Just what is the basis of the argument that Big Government is inevitable, and ever greater Washington control inescapable?

The stream of dialectics begins with a full agreement that "of course" everyone desires strong, dynamic local government in the communities and in the states of the United States. The Big Government apologists never question that proposition. We are told that these are "fine ideals"—the ideal of home rule, the ideal of a flourishing community and state government. Following close upon this disarming prelude, however, it is said that the complexities of modern living make this older ideal merely nostalgic. Our technical society, so they say, has made it obsolete and unworkable. The airplane, the telegraph, the telephone, swift transportation both within the United States and throughout the world make it regrettably necessary that the older ideal give way to the facts of modern life. Over and over again the story is repeated of the complex interrelation, the intricacies, the interdependence of American life. The nation has become a most complex fabric quite beyond the comprehension of the ordinary citizen, a fabric no longer separable, and hence national in its every aspect. . . .

Generally speaking this is all true enough. But the conclusion that is drawn from this familiar picture is that since virtually every government problem has become a national problem, therefore every phase of government action must inevitably be administered nationally from Washington. Since—so the argument runs—local administration or state administration is obviously impossible where national interrelation is so complete, therefore Big Government is inevitable. We are told, in short, that Big Government is the price that must be paid for the wonderful technical development of this nation. . . .

In any such discussion as this an important distinction has to be made. It is not new, but it is one that is often overlooked. It is the distinction between a national policy and central administration of that policy.

It is obvious that many problems that once could be dealt with as a matter of local or state policy now definitely require a national policy, determined through congressional action. Problems once predominantly local in their scope and effect now have repercussions on other parts of the country—and the whole world for that matter—that did not exist in an earlier stage in our development. These often require the enunciation of a national policy and expenditure of federal funds.

But because the central government through the Congress must and should determine upon a national policy in a particular field, it does not by any means follow that *the administration of that policy* must necessarily also be on a nation-wide basis. This distinction between a centralized or national policy and the decentralized or localized administration of that national policy, is a distinction of fundamental importance. It is, moreover, a distinction the apologists of Big Government so frequently and persistently overlook. It is a distinction which unless observed and respected by corrective action in the way of decentralized administration of national policies can lead to the progressive atrophy of most local and state governmental functions.

The distinction between authority and its administration is a vital one. For a long time all of us—administrators, citizens, and legislators—have been none too clear on this point. We have assumed that, as new powers were granted to the government with its seat at Washington, these powers therefore must also be administered from Washington. We have taken it for granted that the price of federal action was a top-heavy, cumbersome administration. Clearly this is not true. The problem is to divorce the two ideas of authority and administration of authority.

Effective techniques of decentralization—not better ways to centralize—should claim our first attention. The very first question we should ask ourselves is: Why cannot these federal activities be decentralized; if not in whole, why not in part? The problem of first concern we must ever keep in mind is: Does this or that federal program really have to be centralized and to what extent? Here is the real job to which our students and experts in public administration and our members of Congress should address themselves. It is a continuing, day-by-day task requiring the focus of administrative and legislative attention upon every opportunity for decentralization as it comes along.

The TVA is a concrete demonstration that ways and means can be devised to decentralize the administration of many of the functions of the central government. Indeed, one of the public's chief interests in TVA these days is as practical, living proof that despite the interrelation of our vast country, despite the need for national policy on many matters heretofore local, the actual carrying out of those national policies can effectively be placed in the hands of local community and state agencies and instrumentalities. TVA's methods of decentralized administration may well prove to be the most important single product of the experiment in the Tennessee Valley. . . .

During a period of American history when centralization of administration in Washington has increased at a rapid rate, in the Tennessee Valley state and local functions of government have grown, in diversity and strength, more rapidly than in any other region of the United States during the same period.

The record of TVA's more than sixteen years demonstrates that in the broad federal field of development of natural resources—of river, land and farm, forests and minerals—there is a reasonable and workable alternative to centralized administration from Washington. The widespread approval of the TVA among the people of the Tennessee Valley region is attributed by the people themselves laregly to this method of decentralization. . . .

Overcentralization is tempting to many. It has a special appeal to the administrator who quite conscientiously sees the complexity of his job in a coast-to-coast responsibility. The oversimplifications and the uniform rules and regulations which centralization encourages, are convenient for him, however inconvenient it may be for the public.

There are those in Congress and among federal administrators who quite genuinely doubt whether they can discharge the federal responsibilities for nation-wide programs and for federal funds (such as those in aid of education) if they must rely upon local units of government over which there does not exist the authority to hire and fire and to set and enforce Washington "standards."

It seems to me however that as against the folly of centralized administration the risks involved in delegations and agreements with state and local agencies seem clearly preferable. Indeed, are not these risks implicit in our democratic faith?

Nor should we overlook the deeper question of how we can help our state and local government gain in competence and in capacity. Surely we should not encourage state and local governments to escape from their duties or abdicate their responsibilities to Big Government, for this is a process that perpetuates whatever are the local weaknesses.

To turn administration of localized problems over to Washington on the ground that thus we escape the inefficiencies and political shenanigans of state and local communities, is nonsense. It merely transfers the political pressures from local into federal political channels. Moreover, centralization to avoid unsavory local influences surely deprives the people of the chance to draw their issues locally and to clean up their own local inadequacies. The fundamental solution is to crowd more, not less responsibility into the community. Only as the consequences of administrational errors become more localized, can we expect citizens to know which rabbit to shoot.

Overcentralized administration is not something simply to be made more palatable, more efficient, and better managed. It is a hazard to democracy. It is a hazard to freedom. Centralization at the national capital or in a business undertaking always glorifies the importance of pieces of paper. This dims the sense of reality. As men and organizations acquire a preoccupation with papers, they become less understanding, less perceptive of the reality of those matters with which they should be dealing: particular human problems, particular human beings, actual things in a real America—highways, wheat, barges, drought, floods, backyards, blast furnaces. The facts with which a highly centralized institution deals tend to be the men and women of that institution itself, and their ideas and ambitions. To maintain perspective and human understanding in the atmosphere of centralization is a task that many able and conscientious people have found well-nigh impossible.

Many administrators recognize this simple truth. But we are so prone to accept Big Government, to improve and refine it at the center to the sad neglect of the periphery where the people live and work, that the federal administrator who tries to reverse the trend is hailed as the exception to the rule. I cite one noteworthy illustration—there are many more. The [former] Secretary of the Interior, Honorable J. A. Krug, has urged the creation of a decentralized regional agency, to aid in the unified development of the Columbia River Valley. In explaining the decentralizing consequences of this proposal Secretary Krug has said: "Final decisions would be made here in the Northwest instead of in my Department in Washington. I would like to give up some of my power and authority exercised at Washington and see it exercised here." In such a spirit of self-imposed restraint among administrators and in Congress lies the road to a workable alternative to Big Government.

Big Government will get bigger and more highly centralized unless there is a conscious, continuous, creative administrative and legislative effort to reverse the trend. The community's impulse to hand its local problems over piecemeal to one remote agency after another, feeds this hazardous push toward Big Government. The surrender of local responsibility for a part of the community's function generates further local weaknesses which furnish the reason for yet another surrender. Local communities and state governments can help by resisting these temptations to take the easy way out. They can help the administrators of federal programs to work out the methods of decentralization case by case.

Those who believe devoutly in the democratic process should be the first to urge the use of methods that will keep the administration of national functions from becoming so concentrated at the national capital, so distant from the everyday life of ordinary people as to wither and deaden the average citizen's sense of participation and partnership in government affairs. For it is this citizen participation that nourishes the strength of a democracy.

THREE WAYS TO LIVE UNDER THE WELFARE STATE [5]

We are moving, as we all know, to a world very different from nineteenth century Victorianism. . . . I need not tell you what are the promised characteristics of this new age, and of this new state. It is what, for convenience, is quite usefully described as the welfare state, a state responsive to the material needs of all its subjects; providing complete and adequate security against all the sinister contingencies of life; abolishing want and unemployment; giving education up to university standard (and beyond) to all who desire to avail themselves of it. In short it will be what I recently saw described somewhat derisively . . . as the Santa Claus state. I have also heard it depicted, with even more derision and cattiness, as a world in which the entire population will have breakfast in bed. It will also be a world in which the state, directly or at one remove, assumes responsibility for the conduct of the major basic industries; a world also in which economically the individual will have largely disappeared. Society indeed has already undergone

[5] From "Economics: Yesterday and Tomorrow," an address by Sir Alexander Gray, C.B.E., Professor of Political Economy and Mercantile Law, University of Edinburgh, delivered before the Economics Section of the British Association for the Advancement of Science, Newcastle upon Tyne, September 1949. *Advancement of Science.* 6:233-43. October 1949. Reprinted by permission. This selection is only a small portion of an address which deserves reading by a wide audience. —Editor.

a process of coagulation, so that, if we count for anything at all, we count solely as a member of our appropriate group. Moreover, let us not forget that these groups may have conflicting interests.

Now in such a changed world where many things, if not all things, will have been made new, the politico-economic problem may be very different from that to which we older people have been accustomed. By the politico-economic problem I mean the problem of how to live together (always a difficult matter) and how to keep things going. It may seem a perverse thing to say; but just as life in heaven (or in some heavens) may not be altogether easy, so possibly life in the agreeable world of the future may present peculiar difficulties of its own.

There are, I think, three ways in which we may manage to live together in the complete welfare state; or perhaps it would be better to say that there are three preliminary conditions, any one of which, if satisfied, would enable us to do the trick.

I. *Compulsion*: The first is that of relying on a degree of compulsion vastly greater than we have yet had the courage or the honesty to admit may be necessary. I am not now pointing out the horrors of the road to serfdom, or of what awaits you when you come to the end of the road. In its higher altitudes this is already a well-discussed topic. I confine myself to the superficial and indeed the platitudinous. A state cannot undertake to provide from under the counter whatever anyone may need unless simultaneously it sees that someone is putting under the counter what is required for the purpose. The state cannot promise every school child a glass of milk at eleven o'clock, unless it has directly or indirectly the corresponding number of cows standing at command. May I refer you to John Ruskin, a writer whom ordinarily I would not commend for his economic insight? "Finally I hold it for indisputable that the first duty of a state is to see that every child born therein shall be well housed, clothed, fed and educated, till it attains the years of discretion." (So far, an excellent definition of the welfare state, even if its concern with welfare is limited to the years of indiscretion.) "But," he goes on, "in order to the effecting this the government must have an authority over the people of which we now do not so much as dream." It ought to be fairly obvious that the state cannot guarantee everyone against want, unless it reserves the right, if need arises, to take anyone forcibly and pack him off to Caithness or Cornwall to do whatever requires being done there. And sooner or later the time may, probably will, come when it will have to realize that it must not be too mealy mouthed or timorous about the exercise of these powers of compulsion with which, on Ruskin's view, the welfare state must arm itself. The state cannot give what is not there. Indeed, in a sense the state, of itself, cannot guarantee anything or any standard of life. It is an old criticism of the anarchists that the state is forever sterile. Properly understood, it is an entirely true statement. It can act only through its subjects; and in this matter of distribution, it can only redistribute what its nationals produce or what can be got from other nations in exchange for their products. And if plague comes, fortified by the Colorado beetle, potato disease, foot and mouth disease, blockade by the enemy and all the other horrors in the Malthusian repertory, a government guarantee of a standard of life will get you nowhere. The power of the government to give is forever limited by what the people themselves produce.

Indeed in this matter I am inclined to carry my pessimism still further. It is the tritest and most hackneyed of platitudes that rights must forever be accompanied by duties; but though we invariably pay lip service to the well-worn dictum, in fact our eyes in these days are morbidly fixed on our rights, whereas our duties, after a vague and perfunctory wave of the hand in their direction, are allowed to fade into the background. The Universal Declaration of Human Rights is in this respect an illuminating document. Now in the economic field a right is something that you get from someone else, whereas a duty is what we do for another. And a society in which each member concentrates on getting rather than on giving has lost the roots of its stability.

If then, in the words of the Universal Declaration of Human Rights, the welfare state is going to provide every one "a standard of living adequate for the health and well-being of himself and of his family, including food, clothing, housing" and much more, it must, in the last resort, have power to compel its subjects to see to it that the national bins are kept full, and that there are ample reserves under the counters of the national stores. . . .

II. *Incentive*: So much for the first method of meeting the future, the method of compulsion and direction—that degree of authority over the people of which John Ruskin alone was capable of dreaming. You do not like it? No more do I, though I am of a more submissive disposition than most. But economically, it might be an efficient system, if the rest of the population were as submissive as I am, which probably they are not. From all we know of the Incas and the Jesuit settlements, it might be for certain placid peoples a highly efficient system indeed, producing on the material level a remarkably high degree of comfort and well-being. If compulsion is to be condemned, it must be on moral rather than on economic grounds; it is to be abhorred, above all, because it involves a denial of personality and an abrogation of responsibility.

But if, disliking the idea of a world resting on compulsion, you ask for an alternative which will preserve our free society, I suggest, as the second of my possible devices for the future, that you might consider what can be done towards a solution of the age-long question of incentive. And in some ways this is the most urgent of all our industrial problems, for never . . . has the clarion-call to work sounded so insistently as today. The idea of "Incentives," however, seems to involve the acceptance of the view that the natural man does not love work, or that he does not love it or endure it cheerfully, except in moderate doses. Yet apparently this innocuous proposition seems to be one which it is rather dangerous to advance in certain circles. For moralists tell us that we ought to love our work, and tend to think that if we have not yet reached that stage, the fault lies not in man, but in the organization of labor. . . . As you may have discovered in your miscellaneous reading, any suggestion that mankind as a whole have in their makeup a something which leads them to regard work as no more than a second-best way of passing the time, is at times roundly described as a foul slander on our fellow-men. . . .

Work, for the present, then, I assume to be something which soon comes to be avoided, except for a small happy section of the community whose work and whose play merge into each other —the small body of insincere cranks who in *Who's Who* describe their recreation as "More Work." We work because we must; we consent to do more work, because of additional inducements and incentives. But in the new world to which we are moving the question of incentive, of overcoming man's disinclination to work, will of necessity become vastly more difficult, just because the older incentives in their harsher form must become enfeebled as we seek to guarantee security and a reasonable standard of life in all circumstances.

Doubtless the problem of incentives should be considered along with the allied question of the removal of disincentives, if we may lapse into the barbarous jargon of these times. I am not sure that the authorities realize how powerfully in certain circumstances the present income tax arrangements operate to restrict effort. The fact that payments in respect of overtime may bring into the group that pays income tax a worker who would otherwise be exempt leads him to assign the whole of the tax exclusively to that portion of his earnings that comes from the extra hours worked. He complains that whereas he has from time immemorial been paid time-and-a-half for work outside normal hours, he is now being fobbed off with three-quarters time: he is in fact being paid at a lower rate for his overtime than for his ordinary day's work. There is of course a catch in it; but if you discuss the matter with him, unless you are a very good dialectician, he has a fair chance of persuading you that he is right.

Waiving the question of the removal of such "disincentives" which I mention merely to complete the picture, it remains true and regrettably true, that the only effective incentives are of a material character, with an appeal to the individualistic and competitive instincts of mankind which we are supposed to be eradicating. You may ring the changes on higher rates of pay and ingenious bonus payments; you may bring in shorter hours; but you are still moving on the material plane and appealing in one way or another to the desire of gain and comfort. Nor do you escape (entirely, or at all) this material character by giving better seats at the opera, or tours to the northern capitals, on the *Kraft durch Freude* [Strength through Joy] principle. And as I said, precisely because we are moving into a better world, this problem of incentive must become more difficult; it may indeed turn out to be the acid test of the stability of our future economy. We have the firmest assurances that the government will in future accept the task of maintaining full employment, though doubtless "full employment" may be variously defined. The testing time which will reveal whether the state has at all times and in all circumstances the power to fulfill this undertaking still lies ahead. But if full employment is defined, as it sometimes has been defined, as a world in which there are more jobs than men, then I tremble as in the presence of a nightmare. . . .

In a world where there are *more* jobs than men, it is fairly obvious that two things will happen. Firstly, and by definition, a number of jobs will remain unfilled, and it is not difficult to say which jobs these will be. [Men] . . . will avoid those tasks which, for any reason, are regarded as unattractive, unpleasant or unduly arduous, though it may quite possibly be that without these a city may not stand. And simultaneously, higher up the scale, employers in desperation will spend their days enticing away the employees of others by the offer of higher wages. . . .

It is sometimes instructive to see on a small scale what may later happen on a larger. Today you have a fairly good illustration of a world of more jobs than men, if you take the market for domestic service. Domestic servants, so far as they survive, having read their Bernard Shaw, make a bee-line for widowers' houses—elderly widowers, with no children about the place. I do not blame them; I should do the same myself. An elderly widower who spends all his evenings at the club provides a haven of peace compared to anything that can be offered by a harassed young woman with four children. Also the elderly widower is more squeezable in money matters. At present, accordingly, the survivors of the race of domestic servants flock to the houses of those who in many cases might be better dead, and avoid those homes where the need is the sorest. This is almost a parable of what would take place in a world of more jobs than men; and the only possible remedy is clear. If there is a danger that certain essential tasks may remain undone because no one is willing to undertake them, the state, even if professedly shunning compulsion, would have to devise means of coercion. And so by another route, you are brought back to compulsion which we have already considered. . . .

Am I perverse in sometimes feeling that today we are tending to be far too impatient of any suggestion of inequality in any sphere of life? I am still enough of a Saint-Simonian (and for that matter, a Fourierist) to consider that it is only by admitting a certain measure of inequality, something of the nature of a hierarchy, that we shall be able to get anywhere at all, or be able to make the machine march. The only place where there is absolute equality (just as it is the only place where there is absolute security) is in the grave. There is, I think, no harm in a certain degree of inequality, on two conditions: firstly, that the resultant disparity should not be offensive; and secondly, that there should be no barrier in the way of the somewhat-less-favored of today becoming the somewhat-more-favored of tomorrow by their own efforts, and (admittedly) by such an admixture of luck as you will never eliminate from life. Life always has been, and always will be, something of the nature of a race; and the young at least would have it so. But there is not much fun in taking part in, or in watching, a race where in advance the umpires impose handicaps which will effectively ensure that all the competitors will arrive simultaneously at the winning-post.

In fact incentives won't work, unless you are prepared to allow some inequality of one kind or another. And there is this further point. We turned to the possibility of devising effective incentives, in order to avoid compulsion and to preserve our free society. But indeed though Liberty and Equality have been for a century and a half yoked with Fraternity in a curious and uneasy trinity, nevertheless Liberty and Equality are natural enemies. . . . For if we are to be free, and if we exercise our freedom, we must be free to be, among other things, unequal. On the other hand, if we are to be equal, it will only be because we are forcibly compelled to be equal, and denied the liberty of surpassing our fellows.

I have offered you compulsion; but you say that if possible you would prefer to retain your freedom. I have suggested that you endeavor to solve the question of incentive in a free society; but you tell me that there may be something illogical in our new society in relying on incentives which, at their worst, . . . are unlovely, and which are of necessity material in their nature, with an individualistic appeal, inevitably differentiating if not dividing men.

III. *A Higher Type of Morality*: The third course . . . is to enroll yourself frankly among the followers of Lenin (for this purpose) and wait in faith for the emergence of a better man, for the universal prevalence of a higher order of morality than that now to found among us; when in consequence the worker will no longer (the words are Lenin's) "calculate with the shrewdness of a Shylock whether he has not worked half an hour more than another, whether he is not getting less pay than another"; when "the necessity of observing the simple fundamental rules of human intercourse will become a habit." Admittedly this is a long-term policy and a long-term hope, and postulates, in the words of Lenin, "a person unlike the present man-in-the-street."

How far we can make ourselves fit to live in a better world by evolving a higher type of morality is presumably not an economic question. Nevertheless I may not omit it today, because in the past . . . it has so often been hoped that our economic difficulties would be solved in some such way. Nearly all our ardent reformers have confidently trusted that in a better world where all things are held and operated on behalf of the community, a higher order of morality would prevail. When workers could feel that they were working for their fellow-workers and not merely for the gain of another, they would adopt a new code of behavior. Admittedly it will be a slow process, even on Lenin's own showing; and therefore perhaps we should not be impatient. . . . Also we have made doubtful progress towards industrial peace; for apparently employment by the state or by a National Board does not necessarily mean bliss and content for all concerned. There is a devastating sentence in the second annual report of the Coal Board. It tells with restrained gratification that there were no official strikes during the year; "but," it adds, "there were 1,635 unofficial strikes where men stopped work in defiance of their union." One thousand six hundred and thirty-five! One is reminded of the love affairs of Don Juan: "And in Spain, a thousand-and-three." Here surely, in the cold statistics of the Coal Board is an illuminating figure significant of the economic and psychological friction prevailing in our society. It will assuredly take some time before we are all prepared to crucify self to such an extent as will qualify us for admission to Lenin's heaven.

And so I leave it—somewhat inconclusively, like certain modern composers who end without even asking a question, but merely because they have exhausted their time or their paper. Compulsion, shall we say, is detestable and ultimately immoral. Incentive is essentially a species of bribery, relying on the competitive instincts and leading us back to what some would have us regard as the jungle of individualism. I am all for the evolution of a better man, and for that matter of a better woman; but it is a slow process for frail creatures whose years are three-score-and-ten. Perhaps in the end there *is* a conclusion, though it is not an economic one. It is that before we can be trusted to live in the New Jerusalem, we must first of all be fit to walk the streets of the New Jerusalem. And as applied to our transitional times, I would suggest that despite all superficial appearances, the New World into which we are moving is not going to be a world which will make everything easy for everybody by giving everybody everything. If it is to work, it will be a world which will make vastly greater demands on every one. It will demand that most difficult of all things to attain, that plant of very slow growth, a higher standard of public and private morality in all things, and in particular the suppression of self. For socialism is parading under a false name, unless it means an order of things in which we forget ourselves in our zeal for the good of society and of our fellows, and in which speculation as to our place in the queue is the last thought that occurs to us. And it is not I, but Lenin, who says so.

BIBLIOGRAPHY

An asterisk (*) preceding a reference indicates that the article or a part of it has been reprinted in this book.

BOOKS AND PAMPHLETS

Aly, Bower, ed. Welfare state: the twenty-fourth annual debate handbook. 2v. Lucas Bros. Columbia, Mo. '50.

Anderson, Maxwell. Guaranteed life. (In brief. v4, no2) 10p. Foundation for Economic Education. Irvington-on-Hudson, N.Y. '50.

Ball, J. H. Where does statism begin? (National economics problems. no434) 34p. American Enterprise Association. 4 E. 41st St. New York 17. '50.

Benn, Ernest. Rights for robots. (In brief. v4, no3) 11p. Foundation for Economic Education. Irvington-on-Hudson, N.Y. '50.

Blake, W. R. Address before the American Cotton Manufacturers Institute, March 31, 1950. Mimeographed text available from the National Cotton Council. Memphis, Tenn. '50.

Brewster, Owen and Humphrey, Hubert. Are we depending too much on government for general welfare? (Town meeting, v 15, no27) 24p. Town Hall, Inc. 123 W. 43d St. New York 18. '49.

Bruehl, Charles. State and the people. 26p. Central Bureau Press. 3835 Westminster Pl. St. Louis 8, Mo. '50.

Byfield, R. S. and LaFollette, C. M. Are we drifting toward socialism? (Reviewing stand. v 14, no 16) 11p. Northwestern University Radio Dept. Evanston, Ill. '50.

Chamber of Commerce of the United States. Drive for a controlled economy via pale pink pills. 23p. The Chamber. Washington 6, D.C. '49.

Chamber of Commerce of the United States. Socialism in America. 74p. The Chamber. Washington 6, D.C. '50.

Clinchy, R. J. Two paths to collectivism. (In brief. v3, no2) 10p. Foundation for Economic Education. Irvington-on-Hudson, N.Y. '49.

Committee for Economic Development. Uses and dangers of direct control in peacetime. 27p. The Committee. 444 Madison Ave. New York 22. '49.

Douglas, H. G. and others. What is the difference between socialism and social welfare? (Town meeting. v 15, no39) 16p. Town Hall, Inc. 123 W. 43d St. New York 18. '50.

Douglas, T. C. Canadians find security with freedom (Cooperative Commonwealth Federation in Saskatchewan). 31p. League for Industrial Democracy. 112 E. 19th St. New York 3. '49.

Eldean, Fred. Trend of socialization. 11p. Fred Eldean Organization. 670 Fifth Ave. New York 19. '50.

Fairless, B. F. Detour ahead. Address delivered before the Baltimore Association of Commerce, April 21, 1950. 13p. Mimeographed text available from the United States Steel Corp. 71 Broadway. New York 6. '50.

Federal Security Agency. The Administrator's report (from the annual report), 1949. 32p. Supt. of Docs. Washington, D.C. '50.

Flynn, J. T. The road ahead. 160p. Devin-Adair. New York. '49.

Flynn, J. T. and Douglas, P. H. What's the road ahead? (American forum of the air. v 13, no 10) 11p. Ransdell, Inc. 810 Rhode Island Ave. Washington 18, D.C. '50.

Garnett, A. C. Freedom and planning in Australia. 331p. University of Wisconsin Press. Madison, Wis. '49.

Haake, A. P. and Krueger, Maynard. Do we want the welfare state? (Reviewing stand. v 14, no 18) 11p. Northwestern University Radio Dept. Evanston, Ill. '50.

Harris, S. E., ed. Saving American capitalism. 373p. Knopf. New York. '48.

Hazlitt, Henry and others. Do current events indicate greater government regulation, nationalization, or socialization? 43p. Economic and Business Foundation. New Wilmington, Pa. '48.

Heaton, Herbert and Johnson, Alvin. Socialism in western Europe. (Headline series. no71) 62p. Foreign Policy Association. 22 E. 38th St. New York 16. '48.

Humphrey, H. H. The welfare state—a state of the general welfare. Address delivered before National Conference of Social Work, April 24, 1950. Mimeographed text available from the Conference. 82 N. High St. Columbus 15, O. '50.

*Humphrey, H. H. and Dulles, J. F. Addresses before the Harvard Law School Forum, Cambridge, Mass., March 24, 1950. Mimeographed texts available from the speakers. '50.

Johnsen, J. E. British socialism today. (Reference shelf. v22, no 1) 287p. H.W. Wilson Co. New York. '50.

Johnson, R. W. Welfare capitalism versus the welfare state. 24p. Johnson & Johnson. New Brunswick, N.J. '49.

Krueger, M. C. Socialism, the answer to capitalism. Address delivered to Socialist National Convention, Detroit, Mich., June 5, 1950. Mimeographed text available from the Socialist Party. 303 Fourth Ave. New York 10. '50.

Laidler, H. W. British labor as government and as opposition. 37p. League for Industrial Democracy. 112 E. 19th St. New York 3. '50.

*Laidler, H. W. Labor governments at work. 23p. League for Industrial Democracy. 112 E. 19th St. New York 3. '48.

Laidler, H. W. Toward nationalization of industry. 32p. League for Industrial Democracy. 112 E. 19th St. New York 3. '49.

Lauterbach, A. T. Economic security and individual freedom: can we have both? 178p. Cornell University Press. Ithaca, N.Y. '48.

*Lehman, H. H.; Reuther, W. P.; Ewing, O. R.; and Meany, George. Addresses delivered before the 45th Anniversary Luncheon, League for Industrial Democracy, April 15, 1950. Mimeographed texts available from the League. 112 E. 19th St. New York 3. '50.

Lewis, E. L. The individual and society. 111p. Exposition Press. New York. '49.

*Lilienthal, D. E. This I do believe. 208p. Harper & Bros. New York. '49.

Lonigan, Edna. Expanding welfare in a free economy. (National economic problems series. no431) 44p. American Enterprise Association. 4 E. 41st St. New York. '49.

Morley, Felix. Power in the people. 293p. Van Nostrand. New York. '49.

Phelan, Towner. Liberalism stands for freedom. (In brief. v3, no3) 15p. Foundation for Economic Education. Irvington-on-Hudson, N.Y. '49.

Pound, Roscoe. Rise of the service state and its consequences. 34p. Economic and Business Foundation. New Wilmington, Pa. '49.

Rosenfarb, Joseph. Freedom and the administrative state. 273p. Harper & Bros. New York. '48.

Russell, Bertrand. Authority and the individual. 79p. Simon & Schuster. New York. '49.

Russell, Dean. Wards of the government. (In brief. v4, no 1) 15p. Foundation for Economic Education. Irvington-on-Hudson, N.Y. '50.

Sutch, W. B. New Zealand's labor government at work. 32p. League for Industrial Democracy. 112 E. 19th St. New York 3. '40.

*Taft, R. A. The individual and his government. Address before the Chamber of Commerce of the United States, Washington, D. C., May 1, 1950. Mimeographed text available from the Chamber. '50.

Thomas, Norman. Why Americans should be Socialists. Address delivered to Socialist National Convention, Detroit, Mich., June 8, 1950. Mimeographed text available from the Socialist Party. 303 Fourth Ave. New York 10. '50.

*Truman, H. S. Message to Congress on Reorganization Plan no27, May 31, 1949. Mimeographed text available from the White House. Washington, D.C. '50.

United States. Economic report of the President. (together with the Annual economic review by the Council of Economic Advisers) 194p. Supt. of Docs. Washington, D.C. '50.

United States. Library of Congress. The welfare state, the case for and against. 69p. (Public affairs bulletin. no83) Card Division, Library of Congress. Washington 25, D.C. '50.

*Wallace, H. A. Address before Progressive Party National Conference on Jobs and the Economic Crisis, Cleveland, O. September 17, 1949. Mimeographed text available from the Progressive Party. '50.

PERIODICALS

Academy of Political Science. Proceedings. 24:1-147. My. '50. Freedom and the expanding state (addresses and papers).

*Advancement of Science. 6:233-43. O. '49. Economics: Yesterday and tomorrow. Sir Alexander Gray.

American Affairs. 12:73-80. Ap. '50. The march. Garet Garrett.

*American Bar Association Journal. 36:196-8. Mr. '50. The general welfare clause: does it authorize a welfare state? K. B. Lutz.

American Economic Review. 40:1-12. Mr. '50. Economic way of thinking. H. S. Ellis.

American Economic Review. 40:446-56. My. '50. March into socialism. J. A. Schumpeter.

American Federationist. 57:4-5. My. '50. What's wrong about welfare? George Meany.

American Magazine. 147:17+. Ja. '49. More security for you. O. R. Ewing.

American Magazine. 147:24-5+. Je. '49. We can't thrive on security. K. S. Wherry.

American Magazine. 148:24-5+. S. '49. We need a fifth freedom: freedom from regimentation. H. W. Steinkraus.

American Political Science Review. 41:306-13. Ap. '47. Democracy and socialism in New Zealand. Leslie Lipson.

American Scholar. 17 no3:297-304. [Jl.] '48. Planning and freedom in a democracy. B. J. Hovde.

American Scholar. 18 no4:397-405. [O.] '49. British socialism. C. L. Mowat.

American Teacher. p 12-15. N. '49. The welfare state: do we want it? A. J. Biemiller.

Atlantic Monthly. 185:61-4. Ja. '50. Everybody on relief? A. E. Meyer.

Bar Bulletin (N. Y. County Lawyers Assn). 7:5-10, 8:32-8. Mr., My. '50. New theories of liability. Roscoe Pound.

*Business Week. p53-4. D. 24, '49. When socialism is defeated.

Business Week. p55-62. Mr. 18, '50. Can a socialist Britain survive?

Catholic World. 166:441-6. F. '48. Which leviathan, big business or the state? C. J. Eustace.

Catholic World. 171:99-103. My. '50. Welfare and the welfare state. J. T. Flynn.

Christian Science Monitor Magazine. p5. Ag. 20, '49. Free enterprise adds up. W. H. Wheeler, Jr.

Collier's. 124:16-17+. O. 22, '49. How much government can free enterprise stand? R. A. Taft.

Collier's. 125:13-15+. F. 4, '50. Mr. Welfare State himself. H. M. Alexander and J. R. Slevin.

Collier's. 125:13+. Ap. 8, '50. Is President Truman taking us down the British road? R. A. Taft.

Collier's. 125:34+. Ap. 29, '50. Would you enter a door marked socialism? B. H. Namm.

Commercial and Financial Chronicle. 171:515-17. F. 2, '50. Welfare state spending "on trial." Henry Hazlitt and others.

*Commercial and Financial Chronicle. 171:1201+. Mr. 23, '50. How America is being socialized. R. S. Byfield.

Commonweal. 51:263-5. D. 9, '49. Australian elections. J. G. Murtagh.

Commonweal. 51:475-6. F. 10, '50. Welfare state.

Commonweal. 51:643-4. Mr. 31, '50. The fair deal.

Congressional Digest. 29:1-4. Ja. '50. Welfare and the Constitution.

Congressional Digest. 29:193-224. Ag.-S. '50. Congress and the welfare state (special issue).

*Current History. 18:1-7, 65-70, 129-33. Ja., F., Mr. '50. Bismarck's welfare state. S. B. Fay.

Current History. 18:134-7. Mr. '50. Elections "down under." Alzada Comstock.

Current History. 18:321-6, 29-34. Je.-Jl. '50. Socialism in the United States. H. W. Laidler.

Dun's Review. p24-5+. F. '50. Are we breeding a generation of "securocrats"? M. C. Faught.

*Economic Intelligence. no22:1-2. My. '50. Subsidies and the welfare state.

Economist. 158:694-6. Ap. 1, '50. Cost of welfare.

Foreign Policy Bulletin. 29:1-2. D. 16, '49. Labor defeats down under mark slight shift to right. W. W. Wade.

Foreign Policy Report. 24:50-63. My. 15, '48. Political and economic conditions in the Scandinavian countries. E. C. Bellquist.

Fortnightly Review. 172(ns 166):172-8. S. '49. Welfare state; social services in Great Britain. Elliott Dodds.

Fortune. 37:2-4. Ja. '48. Who's utopian now? democratic capitalism has made good on most of the socialist promises.

Fortune. 39:69-73+. Mr. '49. Socialism by default; how far have we gone and how do we measure it? John Davenport.

Fortune. 41:95-6+. Mr. '50. Wanted: an American conservatism. C. L. Rossiter.

Fortune. 41:80-4+. My. '50. Britain's road back. J. K. Jessup.

Fortune. 41:76-9+. Je. '50. Britain's road down. J. K. Jessup.

Forum. 111:141-7. Mr. '49. Economic planning: by whom? for whom? Benjamin Higgins.

*Freedom and Union. 5:27-32. F. '50. Faith in individual man. J. F. Dulles.

Harvard Business Review. 28:29-44. Mr. '50. Governmental and voluntary programs for security. J. W. Myers.

*Kiwanis. 35:5-6. Ap. '50. Socialism, monster or neighbor? J. W. LaBine.

*Labor and Nation. 6:10-54. Winter '49-'50. Welfare state ideas and practices (special issue).

Labor and Nation. 6:18-38. Spring '50. The expanding state: welfare and democracy (special issue).

*Life. 28:34. Mr. 27, '50. There is another way: Americans can achieve security without relying on the state.

Look. 14:22-3+. Je. 20, '50. Can we afford Truman?

*Mademoiselle. 31:226-9+. Ag. '50. Raising the basic question.

Nation. 169:390-2. O. 22, '49. Sweden: successful semi-socialism. J. Alvarez del Vayo.

Nation. 170:435. My. 13, '50. Britain's road back (reply to article in Fortune).

Nation's Business. 36:33+. F. '48. How dead is the new deal? J. B. Wood.

*Nation's Business. 37:29-31+. Ap. '49. Our rising welfare state. E. P. Schmidt.

*Nation's Business. 38:33-4+. Ap. '50. 150 years of the welfare state. Blair Bolles.

*Nation's Business. 38:39-40+. My. '50. Journey through the "welfare state." Stuart Chase.

Nation's Business. 38:41-3+. My. '50. Police state's jigsaw pieces. E. P. Schmidt.

New Republic. 122:13-15. Ja. 9, '50. Britain's welfare state. Norman MacKenzie.

*New York Herald Tribune. p21. O. 28, '49. Welfare state faces question: how to make security secure? Mark Sullivan.

*New York Herald Tribune. Sec. 10. p 1-64. O. 30, '49. What kind of government ahead; the responsibility of every citizen. (Text of proceedings of 18th annual forum.)

New York Times. p 1+. Jl. 15, '49. Senate gets Murray bill to implement Truman fight on recession.

*New York Times. p3. Ag. 11, '49. Warning to U. S. against "collectivism." (Text of address by H. C. Hoover.)

New York Times. p3. S. 6, '49. Address to farmers and workers, Des Moines, Iowa. H. S. Truman.

New York Times. p2. S. 28, '49. Address to the women of the nation. H. S. Truman.

New York Times. p 15. N. 4, '49. Address at Minnesota centennial celebration, St. Paul, Minn. H. S. Truman.

New York Times. p 10. Ja. 5, '50. State of the Union message to Congress. H. S. Truman.

New York Times. p3. F. 15, '50. Address at Jefferson-Jackson Day dinner, Washington, D. C. H. S. Truman.

New York Times. p3. My. 13, '50. Address at Butte, Mont. H. S. Truman.

New York Times. p 14. My. 17, '50. Address replying to President Truman's cross-country addresses. R. A. Taft.

*New York Times. p 19. My. 17, '50. Text of Democratic party's Chicago platform resolution.

New York Times. p 1. Jl. 11, '50. House plan for cabinet office of public welfare.

New York Times Magazine. p7+. Ja. 25, '48. Vital fact in the battle of ideologies. Francis Williams.

New York Times Magazine. p 10-11. Ap. 18, '48. What is liberalism?

New York Times Magazine. p 11+. My. 16, '48. Are we becoming a laboristic state? S. H. Slichter.

New York Times Magazine. p37+. S. 12, '48. What is an ism? some definitions. D. C. O'Grady.

New York Times Magazine. p 11+. O. 10, '48. Challenge to the conservatives. Chester Bowles.

New York Times Magazine. p 16. F. 13, '49. Planned economy; quotations, comp. by R. G. Whalen.

New York Times Magazine. p7+. Mr. 20, '49. Acid test of the welfare state. Barbara Ward.

New York Times Magazine. p7+. Ap. 3, '49. We must not be afraid of change. R. B. Fosdick.
   Same abridged. Reader's Digest. 55:8-10. Jl. '49.

*New York Times Magazine. p 10+. My. 15, '49. Appraisal of the welfare state. H. S. Commager.

New York Times Magazine. p 12+. S. 25, '49. Appraisal of Britain's welfare state. R. H. Fry.

*New York Times Magazine. p7+. D. 18, '49. Are we headed toward collectivism? H. F. Byrd and P. H. Douglas.
   Same abridged with title "Is the welfare state a menace to America?" Senior Scholastic. 56:10-11+. F. 8, '50.

New York Times Magazine. p9+. Mr. 26, '50. Affirmation of faith in our economy. S. H. Slichter.

Newsweek. 32:sup 14. N. 8, '48. How free will our economy be? Henry Hazlitt.

Newsweek. 34:96. O. 24, '49. Whose welfare? Raymond Moley.

Newsweek. 35:66. My. 29, '50. Fairdeal family at home. Henry Hazlitt.

*Newsweek. 35:88, 92, 96, 96, 92. My. 29-Je. 26, '50. What liberties are we losing? Raymond Moley.

Nineteenth Century and After. 147:295-318. My. '50. Left road for Britain?

Northwestern Miller. p26-7+. D. 6, '49. Socialism or welfare state. H. G. L. Strange.

Reader's Digest. 56:2-19. F. '50. Road ahead. J. T. Flynn.

Reader's Digest. 56:39-42. Ap. '50. Where the menace to freedom lies. B. W. Knight.
    Condensed from Dartmouth Alumni Magazine. D. '49.

*Reporter. 1:28-30. O. 11, '49. Welfare state. Arthur Schlesinger, Jr.

Rotarian. 76:6. Ja. '50. Freedom counts more than you think. A. M. Astbury.

Rotarian. 76:8-11+. F. '50. Free enterprise: are its best friends killing it? Symposium.

Rotarian. 77:12-15. Jl. '50. Let's merchandise security! W. H. Wheeler, Jr.

Saturday Evening Post. 222:10+. N. 19, '49. "Poorhouse state" is the right name for it.

Saturday Evening Post. 222:12. Ap. 1, '50. We're told that voters against socialism were actually for it!

Saturday Evening Post. 222:32-3+. My. 20, '50. Where's Britain going now? Demaree Bess.

Saturday Evening Post. 222:10+. Je. 10, '50. Democrats may go sour on the "poorhouse state" too.

Senior Scholastic. 53:20-1. O. 13, '48. What kind of government do we want? P. A. Knowlton.

Senior Scholastic. 53:20-2. N. 3, '48. Our economic system. P. A. Knowlton.

*Survey. 85:68-71. F. '49. Lest we forget; President Roosevelt's new deal and President Truman's fair deal. A. A. Berle, Jr.

Survey. 85:107-10+. Ap. '49. The human welfare state. W. O. Douglas.

Survey. 85:438. Ag. '49. Coming out boldly in favor of welfare. J. L. Gillin.

*Survey. 86:73-5. F. '50. Turnabout on something for nothing. R. H. Bremner.

Survey. 86:134-5. Mr. '50. Need is an anachronism. J. J. Corson.

Survey Graphic. 36:521-5. O. '47. America's economic choice. George Soule.

*Tax Review. 10:27-32. Je. '49. "Welfare state" at the state level. J. T. Sly.

This Week. p5+. Je. 12, '49. Pitfalls on the middle road. Stuart Chase.

United States News and World Report. 27:34. D. 2, '49. Welfare state or bankrupt state? David Lawrence.

*United States News and World Report. 27:24-5. D. 9, '49. Socialists lose, socialism stays.

United States News and World Report. 27:12-15. D. 23, '49. Australia turns to the middle.

United States News and World Report. 28:35. Ja. 20, '50. What is right in the left. David Lawrence.

United States News and World Report. 28:38-41. F. 24, '50. Big government; new trend in U.S. T. E. Dewey.

United States News and World Report. 28:16-17. Mr. 31, '50. Pattern for industry control.

Vital Speeches of the day. 15:83-7. N. 15, '48. Human liberty; how to lose it. G. L. Hostetter.

Vital Speeches of the Day. 15:236-9. F. 1, '49. Government for the people. M. W. Ball.

Vital Speeches of the Day. 15:301-3. Mr. 1, '49. Which way America? Ruth Alexander.

Vital Speeches of the Day. 15:327-9. Mr. 15, '49. Liberalism; what and where is it? D. R. Richberg.

Vital Speeches of the Day. 15:518-19. Je. 15, '49. Age of the individual; free members of a mighty partnership. D. D. Eisenhower.

Vital Speeches of the Day. 15:553-4. Jl. 1, '49. Pitfalls of a socialized state. C. H. Marvin.

Vital Speeches of the Day. 15:578-81. Jl. 15, '49. Great decisions must be made; address, June 18, 1949. J. F. Byrnes.
Same abridged with title First things come first. Reader's Digest. 55:10-12. S. '49.

Vital Speeches of the Day. 15:708-11. S. 15, '49. Middle way; all our freedoms are a single bundle; address, September 5, 1949. D. D. Eisenhower.

Vital Speeches of the Day. 15:759-63. O. 1, '49. Socialism, the American pattern. E. P. Schmidt.

*Vital Speeches of the Day. 16:98-102. D. 1, '49. Preserve people's rights. J. F. Byrnes.

Vital Speeches of the Day. 16:231-6. F. 1, '50. Blessings of liberty. J. F. Dulles.

Vital Speeches of the Day. 16:270-3. F. 15, '50. Businessmen must face the facts. L. W. Trester.

Vital Speeches of the Day. 16:322-5. Mr. 15, '50. Common man in an uncommon decade. C. M. Shanks.

Washington Post. Sec. II. p3B. S. 9, '49. U.S. pays only half as much per capita as Britain for "betterment." Clarke Beach.
Associated Press report.

Washington Post. Sec. II. p3B. S. 9, '49. "Welfare state" epithet incenses Whitehall. Hal Cooper.
Associated Press dispatch from London.

Washington Post. Sec. II. p2B. Ja. 1, '50. "Welfare state" 50 years a-borning. R. C. Albright.

SPEECH AND DEBATING

Competitive Debate: Rules and Strategy. By G. M. Musgrave. 151p. rev. ed. 1946. $1.25.

Extempore Speaking: A Handbook for the Student, the Coach, and the Judge. By D. L. Holley. 115p. 1947. $1.50.

High School Forensics: An Integrated Program. By A. E. Melzer. 153p. 1940. 90c.

How to Debate. By H. B. Summers, F. L. Whan, and T. A. Rousse. rev. ed. 349p. 1950. $2.75.

Oral Interpretation of Literature in American Colleges and Universities. By M. M. Robb. 242p. 1941. $2.75.

Representative American Speeches. By A. C. Baird, comp. Published annually in The Reference Shelf. Prices vary.

Each volume contains representative speeches by eminent men and women on public occasions during the year. Each speech is prefaced by a short sketch of the speaker and the occasion.

Selected Readings in Rhetoric and Public Speaking. By Lester Thonssen, comp. 324p. 1942. $3.